FINDING YOUR FOCUS ON...

Relationships

FINDING YOUR FOCUS ON...

Relationships

MARCUS D. KING

Finding Your Focus On... Relationships
by Marcus D. King

Cover Design by Atinad Designs.

© Copyright 2012

SAINT PAUL PRESS, DALLAS, TEXAS

First Printing, 2012

The name SAINT PAUL PRESS and its logo are registered as a trademark in the U.S. patent office.

ISBN-10: 0-9854258-0-6
ISBN-13: 978-0-9854258-0-7

Printed in the U.S.A.

Table of Contents

Foreword

What does it take to have the perfect relationship? I am sure there is only One Person who can truly answer that question correctly and that would be God Himself. Whether they are friendships, kinships, or business partnerships, relationships can be very challenging. If you ask couples who have been married for 50 plus years, like I have done, you may get a variety of answers. One common thread that does seem to be woven into the fabric of their successful relationships is focus. The truth is, no one knows what perfect formula works because every person and couple is different. However, if one does not focus on the person(s) one is trying to build relationship with, the chances of a healthy, strong, enduring relationship developing will quickly diminish, leaving only a wish that will not see fruition. It will only become a reality in which you will fall privy to becoming another add-on to the relationship causality rolodex. That is why "Finding Your Focus" is so very important.

Many times when relationships fail it is because too many people begin to focus on the wrong things. We have a tendency as human beings to allow our focus to be drawn to negative things and thoughts, and we need to challenge ourselves to focus on more things that are positive. Our media and society breed so much negativity that it has become even more of a commonplace to celebrate, and focus on the negative statistics of failed marriages, broken friendships, and soured partnerships. That is why this book was written.

This book is the first of many in a series called "Finding Your Focus". We start with "Relationships" because every human being needs relationships. No matter the age, race, creed, background, gender, etc., God created us for relationships. It seems that our culture has been tainted, and we do not know how to value, create, or understand healthy relationships as much as we should. We are building a society that is comfortable with bonding fast, and then breaking up even faster with little to no conscience. This book is designed to help you either focus or refocus on the important relationships in your life. Take a day or as long as you need to meditate on the sections that make you pause. Make sure you do not only have moments of reflection, but also moments of redirection that will be beneficial. Not only should those moments be a benefit to you, but to those you know or will come in contact with where this could affect all parties involved. Then, assign yourself some goals for a day, week, month or year that will assist you in every facet of your relationships.

I thank you for investing in this revolution to change our society, and also to challenge, and improve yourself as an individual. We need, and should aspire to have, relationships that can create a rich, and substantial environment. YOU ARE the reason our world will find its focus on relationships one soul at a time. Now, let's get ready to focus!

Marcus D. King

"Closer To God"

James 4:8: "Draw close to God, and God will draw close to you. Wash your hands, you sinners; purify your hearts, you hypocrites."

In my morning devotional, the first part of the scripture above was the scripture for the day. It was very convicting for me. I had to analyze myself, and ask the question, "Am I as close to God right now as I can be?" The answer was, "No." It's not that I don't love Him. It's not that I don't know His word. It's just that I know I can do better. It's not the fact that I have been living a horrible life by anyone else's standards. I just know I can do better. So, what's the first step in getting closer to God? The scripture says, "Wash your hands, you sinners." Do you have your hands in places where they shouldn't be? Is everything you're doing in your life pleasing to God? Oh yeah? Have you asked Him what He thinks about everything in your life? If you want to be closer, you must get the dirt off of your hands, recognize you still sin (make bad decisions), ask God to give you His kind of heart, and finally you must not be a hypocrite. Hypocrites are those who say they are not struggling when they really are. Tell God, "I have a problem with __. I want You to help me do better in this area." God says if you do that you are being truthful. If you say you are perfect, you are being a hypocrite. That's how you get close to God. Be real with Him. He loves you so much. He won't leave you like you are. Get closer. He's waiting for you to make a move.

Prayer: Dear Lord, forgive me for anything I've done or am doing that is hindering my relationship with You. If there are areas where I need improvement, and I know there are because You are the only perfect being, I ask You to show me. Deliver, set free, draw us closer to You even now. In Jesus' name I pray, Amen.

Questions

1. What are you holding onto that is not allowing you to get closer to God?

2. What habits do you need to change?

3. What do you need to do in order to find your focus on getting closer to God?

4. Find a scripture on which you can focus, one that will remind you God loves you, forgives you, and wants you to get closer to Him. List it here.

"God Bless The Child"

Mark 15:33-34: "At noon, darkness fell across the whole land until three o'clock. Then, at that time Jesus called out with a loud voice, "My God, My God, why have You forsaken me?"

Are you an adult who is still wondering what it would have been like to have had a father in your life? A mother? Are you still wondering why your mother and/or father left your life at an early age? Does your child want to know why you, and the other parent are not together? Do you still feel a sense of abandonment? Jesus felt the same way while hanging on the cross in our text. God turned His back on His Son in the roughest time in His life. Of course, God had a reason to do so. He couldn't stand to look at the sin His Son was carrying and He couldn't stand to see His Son suffer, but He had to for a greater purpose to be achieved later in His life. Are you dating only older men, and staying with them even though they beat you, verbally abuse you, etc? Do you talk to women any kind of way, disrespect them, and never listen to what they have to say? There may be a void in your life where anger or resentment against a parent who may have not been there, or who may have abandoned you lives. Friend, it's not worth you not forgiving them. It is okay to wonder why they left. Jesus asked, "My God, My God, why have You forsaken me?" You can't be unforgiving. Why? They're human just like you. They make mistakes, too. They have to die, too. Imperfect is how humans are. Begin today to ask God to search your heart, and see if there is any void due to the lack of a fulfilling parental relationship. Begin to analyze your child's life through prayer to see if there lies the same or similar void. Begin today forgiving those that are human just like you. No, I don't know how you feel. I don't know what you have endured, but God does. Begin getting to know the Parent (God) that has always been there, and always will be. He loves you. Let Him have His place. Let Him love you, and help you heal today.

Prayer: Dear Lord, I pray for those who have a void, loneliness, pain, confusion, and unforgiveness in their hearts due to the unfulfilled relationships with their parents. Begin healing them today. Holy Spirit, break through the spirit of those who don't even realize this is, and has been causing problems in their lives. Show them, and then deliver them. After which, heal them. Heal that child who doesn't have both parents in the household. Protect him/her from resentment and pain. Only You can. In Jesus' name I pray, Amen.

Questions

1. If that person who left you came back in your life, would you truly forgive him/her as the Lord has forgiven you time after time, no matter the reason for leaving?

2. What is your definition of "forgiveness"? What can be your process to begin your healing and forgiveness of those who left you?

3. What can you tell God about this situation that you think He does not know, but needs to know? Can you be truthful with Him? Do it now!

4. Focusing on your future, how will you allow God to help you heal?

"The Dead Sea"

2 Corinthians 6:14 "Don't team up with unbelievers. How can goodness be a partner with wickedness?"

Do you want the relationships that requires you to be in God's will? The Dead Sea is a sea that has no outlet. Nothing can survive in it. It is useless. So it is with ungodly relationships. If you are single, a clear point God makes in this verse is for believers not to be in dating or marital relationships with unsaved "unbelievers". You can be cool with them, go out to eat with them, and even shop with them, but God says do not be on the same team with them. Why? The King James Version says, "Don't be yoked together with unbelievers." Yokes were used to bind two oxen together to pull in the same direction in order for a field to be plowed for a crop to be planted. It was an orderly process. There was harmony. There was no pulling away, but two animals pulling in the same direction led by the same farmer. Now if you had a horse and an ox yoked together, you'd have two different animals that will pull away from each other because they don't work well together. They have different agendas, and different make-ups. So it is with a believer and an unbeliever. A believer is going to Heaven and an unbeliever is going to hell. God leads a believer. An unbeliever leads himself, and is led by the devil. Now it doesn't matter how sweet they are to you, how good they look to you, how much money they make, or if they treat you better than any Christian ever has. The fact remains that God says, "No." You ask me why? He's the Farmer, and we are His servants. We are His children. Father wants to spare you the pain that you can't see right now. Do you know people who are dating unsaved people? Ask them if they asked God about it! Based on our text, I can guarantee you He didn't tell them to move forward. He does not lie. Don't compromise yourself. Wait on the God-fearing person you have prayed to get. Get an original, not a fake or a copy. Don't try to save them. You can't. Only Jesus can. Trust God to know what's best.

Prayer: Dear Lord, I pray that You will guide Your children in their relationships. Help them not to choose what they want, or what feels good, but help them choose what IS GOOD. For those who are already in relationships not ordained by You, I ask that You begin to challenge them to either change or leave. I pray that You bring direction for those who even date people in other denominations. Give them further guidance in what You want in their lives instead of what they or the world says they need. Thank You, Lord, for Your perfect will. In Jesus' name I pray, Amen.

Questions

1. Did you pray before you decided to be in the relationship with your mate? What did you pray for?

2. If God gave you the relationship that you prayed for, would you lose your focus on Him?

3. Are there factors that urge you to date or want to be married? List them.

4. What actions can you take before and during the relationship that will allow the both of you to be in God's will, and to stay focused on Him?

"A Lily Among Thorns"

Song of Songs 2:2: "Like a lily among thorns is my darling among the maidens."

Are you waiting for that special person to come into your life? Life today has many beautiful women and handsome men from which to choose. The thing is, the only thing attractive about most you meet is the exterior. Don't you hate it when you like the way everything looks, and then they do something you wish they had never done...they speak? Has what someone said just messed up the whole picture for you? I know. I've been down that road several times. God has someone special for you in mind if you have been praying for someone. The thing is, you need to make sure you are being the things you are asking for, or at least trying to be the things you are asking for. A lily is a very beautiful flower, but this lily in our text is found among thorns. Thorns hurt. Maybe what you have been praying for is in arm's reach. You were reaching for a loving, godly, fun loving relationship, right? Well, as you were reaching for it, a couple of thorny relationships came along and scratched you, and poked you, and left scars, didn't they? Don't worry. Keep reaching forward. Once you get your lily in hand, you'll forget about all the thorns that hurt you. Don't settle for a thorn. Go after the lily!

Don't let the thorns discourage you. You have to move slowly in order to get to your lily without being hurt by the thorns surrounding your lily. What you want takes time and skill. Move fast if you want to bleed to death.

Prayer: Dear Lord, give us wisdom to know who is a thorn and who is a lily. Then give us wisdom in how to obtain what You have for us. Please don't let us go after someone else's lily. We don't want to settle for thorns any longer. Help us move slowly in meeting others and developing relationships. We just want to avoid as much drama and hurt as possible. In Jesus' name I pray, Amen.

Questions

1. What things have you requested from God when speaking about your mate?

2. Will these things you have requested to Him really be in one person? Are your standards too high? Will you be able to handle them if He gives them to you?

3. Are you focusing more on a relationship and a house with your mate than on a relationship with Him and your home in Heaven? Why?

4. What can you do now in order to strengthen your relationship with the Lord, and then prepare for your future mate?

"Will You Trust Or Rust?"

Proverbs 31:11: "The heart of her husband safely trusts her."

Why be in a relationship with someone you can't trust? Do you avoid relationships because you don't trust anymore? If your trust level is low, let me help you rebuild it. There are several words in the word trust that will help us: (1) **TRU**. Be true to yourself and ask God to reveal the truth about the character of person you are with now or will be with in the future. (2) **US**. Make sure you and your potential partner or your current partner knows the focus is not on just me, but **US**. When you are a team, you have to learn to trust your teammate in order for the team to succeed. (3) **RUST**. Rust is defined as deterioration because of neglect. If you don't trust, your relationship will soon begin to dry up, get old, and fall apart. That's why you have to learn to **TRUST**. One of my quotes concerning trust is; **"Trust is the oil that keeps the engine of your relationship running. No trust and your relationship will be like a stalled car that overheated on the interstate and may never be repaired."** So you want to be successful in a relationship? It starts with you.

1. Be TRU to yourself. Don't settle for someone who doesn't respect you or see the value in you.

2. Don't just focus on yourself, but have the US mentality. If you, or your mate, focus on "my" needs only, (and you do need to focus on your needs, too) you will lose the big picture, and cheat, neglect, and become argumentative. Think **team**! What's best for the team?

3. Learn to trust God to send you someone who will treat you like He treats you. If that person doesn't come anywhere near that, or the love doesn't resemble His love at all, cut your losses. Don't let your relationship with God **RUST**. It would be a shame to trust a man or woman more than God. Don't fall apart with Him and expect to be together with man/woman.

4. Trust God to handle what you can't. All men are not dogs...maybe just the ones you dated. All women are not tramps. Trust that God has what you are looking for, and then don't treat him/her like your past partner. Give him/her a chance.

Prayer: Dear Lord, we are nothing if we can't trust. Help us to trust You not to send mess into our lives. Help us not to choose people we can't trust. Help our relationship with You never to Rust. Let us start learning to trust by wiping the dust off our Bibles, and hearts, and learning that real love casts out fear. We don't want to be afraid to open up. We trust You to direct our steps, and show us where to, and where not to go. In Jesus' name I pray, Amen.

Questions

1. Have you allowed your relationship with the Lord to rust because of the lack of trust in man? Why?

2. Do you find that you have trust issues with those around you? Does anything trigger it? Is this due to previous relationships? (Family, boyfriend/girlfriend, etc.)

3. Can you allow God to teach, strengthen, and grow your trust levels for Him so you can trust others? How?

4. Can you focus on God's love for you and trust Him to handle what you can't? How?

"Work Through It!"

Matthew 5:23-24 "If your brother has something against you....go and be reconciled."

In his book The Peacemaker, Ken Sande makes the statement, **"Conflict is an opportunity to solve common problems in a way that honors God and offers benefits to those involved."** There are several ways you can handle a situation when you disagree with someone you are in relationship with, whether it be a coworker, family member, or your sweetie with whom you never have had an argument until now. You can choose to be in denial and act like nothing ever happened, you can attack and point out all of their faults and why your little feelings are offended, or you could take the big picture approach. The big picture approach is seeing what behavior God would want from you and behaving in a manner that would make Him proud. We can't run when someone is not agreeing with us because that will make us pushovers. We have to learn to accept people, and their differences. You don't need another you or YOU will never grow. We can't always attack because we will make things worse or cause relationships to be broken that should not be. We need to look and see our fault in it. Then we need to ask ourselves the question "Is what we are in conflict about really important enough for us to give up what we are trying to build together?" Always remember this: expect conflict, but work through, and not around conflict. It's easier to walk away from it than it is to work through it. You grow when you work through it. You run into the same problem in another form if you always run away from it. You destroy relationships when you always attack. Conflict is good because it gives you an opportunity to see if you really want to be where you are. God says you must confront the one with whom you are in conflict in order to restore the relationship. The goal in confrontation is peace...not who is right. Get it right before you get married. Get it right while you are married so you can stay married a long time.

Prayer: Dear Lord, thank You for allowing conflicts to come into our lives. We want to learn how to handle conflict as singles so we can do a better job when we get married. Please don't let people who don't want to work through things get married. They really haven't understood what a real relationship is all about. Help them to work through conflicts the proper way, making You proud and encouraging others before they get married or while they are married. We represent You. Help us be patient with others just like You. In Jesus' name I pray, Amen.

Questions

1. How do you handle your conflicts?

2. Is the root cause of the conflict with the person or the situation you are discussing?

3. Think of a current or recent conflict. Is/was it really important enough for you to give up or jeopardize what you are trying to build together? (In business or loving relationships.) How can you diffuse the situation?

4. What techniques can you create to be a better listener, communicate effectively, and encourage a peaceful result of the conflict?

"Real Love"

Romans 8:38: "And I am convinced that nothing can ever separate us from His love. Death can't, the angels can't, and demons can't. Our fears for today, our worries about tomorrow, and even the powers of hell can't keep God's love away."

There really isn't much I can say about this verse, is there? God puts it to us like this, "Whatever you do, have done, or will do, whatever the devil has tried to do to you doesn't matter. You can't stop My love from protecting you. You can't stop My love from rescuing you." Can't you hear God saying, "Look up at the sky. As far as you can see, and beyond, is how much I love you. Look at the ocean, as far down as you can see, and beyond, is how much I want to provide for you. Don't you know I love you, child? Don't you know I know all about you? Even if you wanted to you couldn't outrun My love. You can't worry away My love. Even if Satan brought all the family of demons against you, My love would build a wall of protection around you so he could only get so close. I know tomorrow and what it holds. Guess what else will be with you tomorrow…My Love. No one can stop Me from blessing you. No one! Now, I have one question to ask you? Will you let Me love you? Then trust Me."

Prayer: Dear Lord, teach me how to receive Your love. Then, teach me how to give Your love away. In Jesus' name I pray, Amen.

Questions

1. Can you really comprehend the definition of "unconditional" love? Are you convinced? Why?

2. How do you experience God's love? How can you express God's love to those who need to know He loves them and has not left them?

3. Has the Lord shown new expressions of His love to you? In what ways?

4. What is the greatest expression of love you can give or show the Lord and to someone you love?

"Less Than 12 Hours"

Ephesians 4:26-27: "Go ahead and be angry. You do well to be angry- but don't use your anger as fuel for revenge. And don't stay angry. Don't go to bed angry. Don't give the devil that kind of foothold in your life."

There are usually twelve hours of your day, from sunrise to sunset- at least in our hemisphere. We spend eight or more hours at work, about eight hours sleeping, and divide the other eight hours between extracurricular activities and family. Now, from the look of your schedule, you need all the positive energy coming in and going out of your life that you can get. It would be a shame to wake up angry, go to work angry, do your extracurricular activities angry, and then lose sleep because you are angry, wouldn't it? God is not telling us to not be angry. Anger is a normal, godly characteristic. He too gets angry. He is telling us we must not sin in our anger. We must first know why we are angry, and then we are to respond to that reason in a way that is pleasing to God. The text reads, "Don't use your anger as fuel for revenge." You must respond, but make sure the motive behind your response is right. "Don't stay angry." God expects you to work your anger out and not carry it around for days or even weeks. "Don't go to bed angry." It sounds as if He desires for us to work this out in less than 12 hours if at all possible. You usually don't get upset right when you get out of bed, so anything after that limits the amount of time you have to get through your anger process. Why?

"Don't give the devil that kind of foothold in your life." If you leave the door to your anger open long enough, the devil will bring in his little friends...resentment, division, jealousy, fear, divorce, fighting, and all the rest of his little critters that will ride on the back of anger into your life. Has someone made you mad? What time is it? The clock is ticking away the time for you to deal with it. Calm down and take a deep breath. Take the high road of maturity and close that door on the situation, enjoying your day, and getting a good night's rest. It is okay to forgive people. That's actually not a sin.

Prayer: Dear Jesus, help us, when situations or people upset us, to admit that we are angry. Then, help us honor You by handling our anger in a godly way so that others watching will recognize that You live in us. In Jesus' name I pray, Amen.

Questions

1. When you become angry, how do you react? Christ-like? Do you draw people nearer to Christ or push them away?

2. Do you have a place or time where you can refuel yourself? If not, why?

3. Are there areas in your life that are stressful? How can you make them less stressful or create a less stressful atmosphere?

4. What actions can you take in the future to prevent past events (anger) from reoccurring??

"Honey From A Dead Lion"

Judges 14:18: "...What is sweeter than honey? What is stronger than a lion?"

Have you ever had a situation that seemed hopeless or endless? Have you lost someone dear to you who was a source of strength and security? Was it a mother, father, sister, brother, friend? Well, Samson had killed a lion here in the text, but bees came by later on and made honey in its carcass. I know it sounds strange, but that's how God works. God can make something sweet come from losing your source of strength. He can use whatever left a bitter taste and bring a sweet taste to your life. All things work together for good. If the lion had not died, Samson would not have had honey. Sometimes, we have to lose some people or things before we fully respect how sweet their lives were to us. Even lions, so strong and powerful, must die, but God has some bees coming to drop joy into your soul that will make their memory oh so sweet. Only God can bring honey from a dead lion. Thank God for the life of your lion. Thank God for the honey He's about to bring to erase the bitter taste that has been left in your mouth by of the loss of your lion. This is dedicated to one of my lions, Marcus Patton. I now can taste the honey in the form of the lives he touched and the friendship we shared. Oh, how sweet it is to feast on the good memories of a lost lion!

Prayer: Dear Lord, bless all those who have a bitter taste in their mouths because of the loss of something or someone they held dear. Bring some joy out of their frustration. Drip some drops of Your honey You call joy into their souls. In Jesus' name I pray, Amen.

Questions

1. Reflecting back, do you have a "lion" in your life that you have not tamed?

2. What are some realistic ways you can tame then kill this lion?

3. Do you feel you can speak to someone who has been in this situation who can give you godly counsel? (Bible Study with open dialogue, friend, counselor, etc.)

4. Focusing on the "honey", how do you picture yourself gaining the sweetness out this situation? (Mending a lost relationship, recalling memories of someone past, etc.)

"More Than A Woman"

Proverbs 19:14: "Houses and wealth are inherited from parents, but a prudent wife is from the Lord."

A woman is simply a female who has grown up to be the age of an adult by society's standard (maybe 18 or 21). A lady is a woman who has learned to respect herself, and others respect her as well, because she has a deep respect for the Lord. A woman can have a child, but it takes a mother, a lady to raise a child the right way. Are you a lady or just a woman? Here's how you can tell: a lady's actions speak louder than her words. She is confident in who she is and lets no one try to change that. A lady thinks a man would be good to have in her life, but really doesn't need a man in her life to feel secure. A lady dresses like a Christmas present; her wrapping looks good and tasteful, making you want to know what is on the inside because you can't see it all. She leaves room for a man's imagination to roam. A lady can talk about you, and correct a problem without you even realizing you were just insulted. A lady knows how to support a man and bring him back to life when he has been wounded. She knows that she has influence, and uses it for her good. A lady works hard on herself, because she sees her value. A lady will sacrifice for her children, and go without so they can have. A lady will love you into what she sees you can be. She will tell you when you're wrong in private, but have your back in public. A lady needs to be treated like a lady. She needs to be told she is appreciated. To all the ladies who read this, some woman needs to know how you became a lady. Teach her. My mama is a lady. You're more than a woman. We men could not make it without you.

Prayer: Dear Lord, only a real lady knows You. Help us to respect Your creation more than we have. Help ladies respect each other. Certainly help me respect ladies. We know You created them to be more than women. Help all women to fulfill all that You created them to be. In Jesus' name I pray, Amen.

Questions

1. Are you a lady or just a woman? If you are not a lady or have been told that you do not carry yourself well, how can you become a lady?

2. If you are a man or a lady who sees a woman, not a lady, how can you give her constructive criticism on how to become a lady?

3. How can you show respect to a female in spite of what level she's on in regards to woman versus lady?

4. How can you focus and/or help females focus on becoming the lady that would make the Lord proud?

"Love Is Kind"

I Corinthians 13:4: "Love is patient and kind..."

Kind: Friendly, generous, or warm-hearted in nature.

How is your love life? I mean, is love a lifestyle for you, or is it something you just do when you feel like it? In order to love in a healthy manner, it must be a lifestyle for us. If that is the case, being kind must be a lifestyle as well. We should look for opportunities to be nice to people. There are so many people who need love every single day and we just bypass them. Why don't we show them love? Usually, we are so focused on where we are going we just use them to get to our next destination. We use the excuse, "I didn't come here to be friends with anyone. This is business!" While it may be business, there is no excuse for having a nasty attitude in the process of conducting business. How did you treat that person who gave you change as you passed through the tollbooth this morning? Did you look at him, smile, and say "thank you" for the change they may have been given to you, and then continue forward? Or did you just take out your 20-dollar bill, not say a word because you were so focused on getting to work, hand it to them, and kept moving? I hear you, though. "They didn't do it to me!" Here's the point: you show love not because the person showed you love, but because kindness is or should be a part of your lifestyle. Make a commitment today to find as many people to be kind to this week. There's the person who takes your order, the person who does your hair, the person who holds the door open for you while you are on your cell phone, or the person who lets you get in front of her in traffic. All it takes is a "Thank You." It takes but half a second to wave your hand to say thank you for letting me get over. How long does it take to give a smile? Lest I make your assignment too simple, smile at those who frown at you. Open the door for those who didn't help you pick up your papers when they fell. Don't retaliate on that person who disrespected you, but keep your cool, and be kind, and don't put on a sarcastic smile. If you can't be kind without doing so, then you have some growing to do in this area. You can never lose when you are kind, because you always know you did the right thing regardless of what happened to you. There's nothing like having a clear conscience! How kind are you? Look for opportunities to improve because your one act of kindness could make a person's day turn from sad to glad. Look at how powerful you are! Now that you know your power, what will you do with it? There's an opportunity for you to be kind as soon as you finish reading this devotional. Take it! If they don't receive it, you win anyway! Do it again!

Prayer: Dear Jesus, help me see how I can improve on loving others by being kind even if they are not kind to me. You have been so kind to me even when I haven't been kind to You. If You can do it, then I want to begin today loving people with kindness who may not deserve it because I know I don't deserve Your kindness all the time either. In Jesus' name I pray, Amen.

Questions

1. When was the last time you passed someone and gave the "hello smile", looked at your cell phone or at the ground in order to avoid speaking? Was that showing love?

2. The last time you gave to your church or a homeless person, or volunteered did you do it with love? Did you do it to receive something in return (Tax write off) or because you felt you had to?

3. Our Best Example showered people love and respect. How can you make His life and example relevant to yours?

4. What areas do you feel you need to focus on when it pertains to being kind to others?

"The Power Of A Father"

Matthew 3:17: "And a voice from Heaven said, "This is My beloved Son, and I am fully pleased with Him."

Can you feel the scene? Jesus is experiencing the most important day of His life. He is getting baptized and is about to graduate into a brand new era of His life. People whom He knows are there, strangers are there, and then out of no where His Daddy makes an entrance. His Daddy's presence would have been great to have all by itself, but He spoke words of affirmation and confirmation to, and about His Child. How powerful that was! Some people didn't have this experience with their fathers growing up and have no idea how that feels. Others did have that experience, and it has given you the confidence you needed from that point until now to achieve more than you could imagine because your father validated you. You pleased him. Fathers have the power to bring security and confidence into the lives of their children. Many people go throughout life with a low self-image, looking to be validated, and kept safe, because they never heard, "I'm proud of you, man; you're beautiful, girl; I love you; you can do and be anything you want in life" from their father. Thank God for the fathers who have stood by their children and spoke into their lives positive nuggets that uplifted them. Those children are stronger and more positive because of it. If your father wasn't there for you physically or emotionally, all hope is not lost. You're about to have some more graduations in your life that you will want to have your father celebrate with you. If your father is deceased, or even if he is distant, you still have the Father of Fathers Who will be there for you. He's looking down every morning you wake up saying, "You're My child, and I am well pleased with you! I'll never leave you because I've always been here with you and will always be there for you! I'm proud of you!" Thank God for your earthly daddy. If you're mad at him, ask God to help you forgive him so you can be in God's will. If he's no longer with you, ask God to help you remember him. If you are a father, ask God to help you be the best one you can be. Most importantly, say thank You to the Daddy who speaks to you everyday. Daddy loves you so much, and He's there for you every time you need Him. Now, when Daddy says you can do it, and you got it going on, what else matters? "Happy Father's Day" every day to the dads here on earth, and to our Father in Heaven.

Prayer: Dear Jesus, thank You for the men who have chosen to become fathers to the children You blessed them to have. Help fathers to continue to be strong and courageous. Help those who are fearful or negligent to grow into their manhood by getting to see how good a father You are. Some son or daughter needs their love and presence. Thank You, Father, for validating me, and showing me Your love so I can find security in You. In Jesus' name I pray, Amen.

Questions

1. How can you have an enhanced relationship with your Heavenly Father?

2. If your father is in your life, how can the relationship with your Heavenly Father spill over in this relationship? If your father is not in your life (deceased or other circumstances), how can you be a mentor or a better father?

3. If you are a woman in a single parent household, how can you show your children that their Heavenly Father loves them in the absence of a father?

4. On what areas will you focus on when praying for fathers or fatherless households?

"The Four Brothers"

Mark 2:3: "Four men arrived carrying a paralyzed man on a mat."

In the movie <u>Four Brothers</u>, men of different cultures and backgrounds come together for one cause: Mama was mishandled. In spite of their contrasting cultures and backgrounds, these men were brothers, and when it was time to stand up for their mother, nothing mattered, but the cause at hand. The same is true for these four men who are in our text today. We don't know their names, where they are from, or even what color they are. I think God left that detail out on purpose to show us that the real point was they had a brother in need of help, and he needed to get to Jesus. It's amazing how people can come together for a highly publicized crisis. We often see hurting, broken people who need our assistance, but it's so astounding how that sympathy wears off after we give our money or volunteer our (1) hour. These four men didn't just get the helpless man to the house where Jesus was. Their job was not complete. They made a way to Jesus for the man and it appears that they didn't leave until the man was up on his feet again. What kind of brother or sister are you? There are people every day who need you and three other people to help them get back on their feet. If a crisis like Hurricane Katrina can take thousands of strangers and put them into apartments, find them jobs, and give them clothes to get their lives back together, that means that there were jobs, clothing, and apartments available before those thousands showed up to that city, but we couldn't get the four brothers mentality in our cities, because we don't see poverty and the poor everyday in our city as a crisis. The sad truth is that many of us humans love to be part of large events until the reality sets in that some people need more than a dollar. These four men made a sacrifice, took a risk, and shared the responsibility of helping one person get his life together. Things are much easier when you have a few more people helping you carry the load. When God speaks to you to help someone, and you feel you can't do it by yourself, it may be that He wants you to find 3 other people to help share the load. Seems to me America has proved that homelessness can be erased. All it takes is a "four brothers mentality" on a daily basis.

Prayer: Dear Jesus, thank You for showing us how to come together during a crisis. Teach us to see the crisis on a day-to-day basis so that we can do a better job of joining with our brothers and sisters to help one another. We all have the same Father, and that's You. Forgive us if we have failed You in this area so that we may do a better job in the future. In Jesus' name I pray, Amen.

Questions

1. Are there organizations that you said you would like to volunteer with, and have not yet done so? Why?

2. What is causing you from not assisting others at all or as frequently throughout the year? (Finances, background check, transportation, time, asking too much of you, etc.) Can you find another way to volunteer?

3. Do you feel that you do not have anything to offer when it comes to assisting others? Have you ever taken a skills assessment to understand your gifts or interests?

4. What are small tasks that you can do in order to assist those around you and make a difference in someone's life now, and then build from there?

"Now What?"

Esther 4:14: "...who can say, but that you have been elevated to the palace for such a time as this?"

Having a relationship is a desire, and goal of many people I come across on a day-to-day basis. Being chosen to be in one is a dream come true. I don't think anyone wakes up, and says, "I think I want to be in a dysfunctional relationship, and then end up broken, and put in a position where I don't trust like I used to trust." I think sane people have a picture of being chosen by someone who admires them. No woman wants to be with someone who is a lowlife if she values herself. Every woman I know wants a king. So did Esther. She got herself together, and was pleasing to the eye of the king, and he chose her over every other woman. She found out what the king liked, and reeled him in! Once she had her new man, however, her uncle who had raised her let her know that even though she now lived in a palace, she shouldn't forget why God gave her that kind of man. That she should remember the reason she was with him was because his last relationship ended; not because of looks, but because of flawed character. Your looks may get him, but your character determines whether he stays. You are with him because God has a bigger plan for you than just feeling good, sleeping on fine linens, and pointing your finger in the face of those who didn't get chosen. God has placed him in your life, and put you in this position, so He can use you greater than you have ever been used before. Now that you have a man, now that you are in position, what will you do with it? God will let a Queen or

King desire you at the right time. Make sure you know God has more than a relationship on His mind! If not, the process may take longer until you recognize that. Got the relationship you desired finally? Now what?

Prayer: Dear Jesus, thank You for knowing my desires. Help me to remember that relationships from Your point of view are ministries that draw me closer to You, and are not meant to take me away from You. I want to be in Your will so it can last, and be healthy. In Jesus' name I pray, Amen.

Questions

1. Are your desires for a relationship consistent with what the Lord desires for you?

2. What are the priorities you feel should be in your relationship?

3. If you are single, are you ready for, and will you respect the ministry (union) God designed for you? If you are married, in what areas can you improve to have the ministry the Lord has designed for your marriage?

4. How can you focus on those areas you personally need growth in so the Lord can bless you, and your future or current relationship?

"Difficult People"

Esther 7:10: "So they hanged Haman on the gallows he had set up for Mordecai, and the king's anger was pacified."

If people really knew how ridiculous it was for them to hate on you, then they would stop dead in their tracks. Let me be clear: if you are not being hateful yourself, and are trying to treat people right, then God may have allowed a difficult person to be assigned to you. Why? That's the way He is going to get you your next promotion. Haman was next to the throne, but he hated Mordecai who was cool with the queen. He hated Mordecai because Mordecai wasn't impressed with people in high places. He respected those who showed respect for themselves and other people. Haman only cared about himself, and talked crazy to everyone else. So, Haman made it his life goal to kill not only Mordecai, but everyone associated with him. He tried to throw dirt on a good man. He listened to his crazy wife, and his crazy friends who told him to make a device that would ultimately be used to kill Mordecai. Little did he know, there was some dirt on him that the king knew about, and the king ended up hanging Haman on the very gallows he had put in place for Mordecai's execution. Guess what happened next? "The king took off his signet ring - which he had taken back from Haman, and gave it to MORDECAI, and Esther appointed Mordecai to be in charge of HAMAN'S PROPERTY ON THE SAME DAY HE WAS KILLED!" (Chapter 8 Verse 2) Crime doesn't pay, but difficult people pay well. The next time someone hates on you, pray for them, but keep in mind that some people are just plain difficult, and won't do right because they have negative thinking, and a jealous heart. Step back and let God deal with them. He knows how to take back things He gave to them, and give them to someone who knows how to handle a blessing - YOU! The next time they act crazy with you, just say to yourself, "You can be that way if you want to!" Then smile, and go on about your business because when people act a fool, and you have done no wrong, that usually is a sign of favor on your life that is about to break loose! THANK GOD FOR DIFFICULT PEOPLE! They help you develop the character to handle what God is about to give you that they couldn't handle themselves, because they were so focused on you. Wise people know not to mess with a child of God.

Prayer: Dear Jesus, I know that You love everyone, so help me to do the same. For those who have hard hearts, I pray even more. Yet, I am prepared to receive all the blessings of those whose attitudes prove they have chosen not to honor You with the responsibility You have given them. Only help me to not be difficult, too. In Jesus' name I pray, Amen.

Questions

1. Besides praying for them, how did you react to those who had been difficult with you? Did it help or hinder the situation?

2. Could you have handled that situation better? How?

3. Instead of listening to others, how can you focus on God's voice when He tells you how to handle the situation?

4. When a difficult person or situation comes, can you focus on the celebration of the fact that the Lord has a breakthrough for you in the midst of it all?

"Refreshing"

2 Timothy 2:22b: "...Pursue faith, and love and peace and enjoy the companionship of those who call on the Lord with pure hearts."

I remember when I used to work out consistently, and would be so very tired, and thirsty. (I'm not the only one who isn't consistent!) After working so hard to get in shape, and sweating profusely, you don't want to put a soda into your system. You want to put something in you that will compliment the goals you have in mind for developing a healthier lifestyle. So, I would leave the fitness center, and find the nearest store. If they wouldn't have my favorite work out drink...a blue Powerade I search stores until I found it. Once I found it, it was so cold, refreshing, I felt replenished inside, and was ready to move on with my day. Life and relationships should be the same way. Paul is telling Timothy to seek relationships with individuals that have the ability to encourage you with their faith, know how to love you and other people, and when you think of spending time with them, a sense of peace comes to your mind. If you are looking to spend time with people, you need to pursue these things in every relationship you may find yourself in. These are the only kind of people who bring strength and vitality to your life. Why spend your life sweating and working to be a person with values, hopes, dreams, and bringing joy to the lives of others, and then take into your life people who have a negative view of life? They only think of themselves, and you really are only around them because you have nothing better to do. That's not refreshing, but depressing! Don't stop at the first person you come to if they don't offer what you desire. Pursue the faith, love, and peace you prayed for in your life. Many times we pray for a refreshing relationship, but can't maintain one. Why? When people begin to pour their love, faith, and peace into our lives, it leaks right through the big hole in our hearts. Ask God to repair your wounded heart, and prepare you to be refreshing, and to receive refreshment. Faith, love, and peace -3 qualities to look for if you want to be refreshed!

Prayer: Dear Jesus, because of the faith You have, the love You show, and the peace You bring to me, I am always refreshed when I spend time with You. Help me have relationships with family, friends, and significant others who share Your qualities. More importantly, help me possess the qualities that I desire so I too can be a thirst quencher. In Jesus' name I pray, Amen.

Questions

1. Do you surround yourself with people who encourage and support you? Why?

2. Why do you entertain those who do not encourage or support you when you are in need, but drain you with their issues?

3. Do you have difficulty understanding healthy relationships? Why?

4. Do you focus on helping (quenching) others, and not replenishing yourself? Why?

"Welcome Home, Sweetheart!"

2 Samuel 6:20: "When David returned home to bless his family, Michal came out to meet him and said in disgust, "How glorious the king of Israel looked today! He exposed himself to the servant girls like any indecent person might do!"

Many men and women find themselves wondering why they are all alone or why someone doesn't want to spend time with them. Many times it's because they do not know how to greet someone. In this story, David had been out working hard in the field. He had success by getting the Ark of the Covenant back, and was so excited that he wanted to rush home, and share the good news with those he loved. He wanted to bless his home. Well, David was dancing in the streets because he had had a good day. There were other women in the streets who were celebrating with him, and there also were other men. They were happy for him, but what does the one person he cared the most about have to say? First, Michal his wife, who was looking at her man, greeted him with a nasty expression of displeasure. Secondly, she didn't ask how he was doing, instead, she immediately points out that he looks foolish dancing in the streets. Thirdly, she sounds jealous, because she only says he looks foolish to the other ladies because he was dancing. What home girl should have done is gotten out of the window she was looking through, run downstairs with excitement because her King was home, danced with him, and let him tell her the exciting news, because it was apparent he hadn't been home in a minute. He had had a rough time away from home, and the last thing he needed was a terrible greeting. At least he did come home. At least he had been out doing what God wanted him to do. Still, he gets a welcome like this. Maybe she was negative and not pleasing in attitude because her daddy Saul, who tried to kill David, couldn't stand to see other people happy either. David wasn't pleased with her reception, and neither was God. Listen to verse 23, "So Michal the daughter of Saul remained childless throughout her life." If you don't want to be alone, know how to welcome someone home! That's a good motto to live by.

Prayer: Dear Jesus, teach us to put aside our opinions, and see how others are doing before we make our judgments. Help us to prioritize what we say so that our relationships will be in order with Your will. I pray that You teach us how to speak with one another so that we will build one another up, and not tear each other down. In Jesus' name I pray, Amen.

Questions

1. How do you welcome those close to you into your home or your presence?

2. When you encounter someone, and you say, "Hello. How are you doing?" do you mean it or is it something you have become accustomed to saying each day? Do you wait for a response?

3. Are your words calming and welcoming to people in person, in your emails, or even on your voicemail?

4. On what area(s) can you focus on to create a welcoming spirit in your voice and body language?

"Check Up On It!"

2 Chronicles 9:1: "When the queen of Sheba heard of Solomon's reputation, she came to Jerusalem to test him with hard questions..."

There is something to be said for a person who jumps into a situation without checking out what they are jumping into. I believe the phrase would be, "Making an emotional decision." As we know, those can get you caught up in some strange places in life. We must take some notes from the queen of Sheba on how to approach a situation before making a judgment on what you heard or thought about that person or place. It says that when the queen "heard of Solomon's reputation", she tested him with "hard questions." When getting involved in relationships, many times we fail to ask the hard questions before we make a commitment for fear of losing the person we are interested in. The queen later gave Solomon gifts after he was able to handle all the questions she had to ask him. The order was as follows: questions, then gifts. Many times we give up gifts, and then we have a lot of questions. Wrong order! You need to have inner peace before you begin to give pieces of you away to people. Get peace by being comfortable with who you are, valuing your time, and making sure you give an entrance exam to all those who want to enroll in the University of YOU. If they pass the entrance exam, they have more tests to take before they graduate and come into your Real World. Be who you are. Don't play games, but you must also guard your heart, and not let someone you've known for 5 minutes or 2 days know all of your business. Before you make that next decision, you'd better listen to queen of Sheba. She heard about his reputation. That means somebody knows him. If you don't know anyone who does, my friend Google will tell it all. He never lies, but only tells the facts. You deserve the best, so make sure you give yourself a chance at something that will last and something you desire, because you were prepared and got some important information early on. Don't you think you're worth that much? Don't go overboard please! That will show more insecurity, and a real lack of trust. You may need counseling rather than a relationship at this time. You have applications for jobs, schools, loans, and other very important aspects of life. If someone can get you with no credit, no background check, and no experience, you may need to slow it down a bit, and re-evaluate your processes. Beyoncé already told you...Check Up On It! Not just how it looks on the outside, but on the inside.

Prayer: Dear Jesus, thank You for discernment and wisdom. Help us to use these two tools when we are embarking upon situations that we have not come across before, whether it is a job, relationship, friendship or any kind of "ship". We need You to open our eyes and help us focus on what You desire for us more than what we desire for ourselves. In Jesus' name I pray, Amen.

Questions

1. Before making important decisions, do you research your information and ask important questions?

2. Although you may not have received all of the information to make a conscience and informed decision, do you move forward anyway? Why?

3. What have you done when you do not have peace concerning the decision you made?

4. How will you focus on controlling your urge to making emotional decisions and having peace with decisions?

"The Relationship Test"

Genesis 19:26: "But Lot's wife looked back as she was following along behind him, and she was turned into a pillar of salt."

When you look back over your life, the relationships you have had with people may have been where you have had your greatest joys or your deepest pains. There is devotion and dedication that is expected from those you trust with your very life. There are deep secrets, dreams, and deep desires that are shared with those you have become fond of. Yet, as much as you have built trust, and companionship, there always will be a time, or many times, when the true strength of your relationship is tested. In these times, you get to see how dedicated a person is to you. Lot had been married to his wife, and had several children. She was about to lose her house and was about to have to leave the city she had grown fond of. She was even told by God's angels to leave the city with her husband. The scripture says that as she was following behind Lot, she looked back.

Some people may be holding your hand, walking beside or behind you, yet their heart is stuck on something from the past. Some people can't move forward with you into new endeavors. They are good people, but they just have reached their growth point. She was so focused on the past that she could not adjust to change, and envision starting something new in the future. The test was a heart check. God sets up situations sometimes so you can see who is with you wholeheartedly, and who is just holding your hand while something else has their attention. Lot obeyed God, and moved on. She looked back, and died where she was. You can either die spiritually, economically, emotionally, educationally with those who don't want to progress forward, or you can do what Lot did. Her choice to look back was the disobedience that led to the ending of the relationship.

Because she disobeyed God, her marriage ended. She crossed the line, and God's warning of that relationship ending came to pass. When you are tested, make sure you choose God over a person, place or thing. Don't be caught having more dedication to what is familiar, and what you think you need than being totally committed to being in the Will of God. Don't choose to live with someone who won't marry you. There's a reason you can't get a full commitment. This story does not support divorce, but wise decisions. It is not limited to dating or marital relationships. It also shows that when we make the wrong choices God sometimes will have to make the hard ones for us. Testing is good. You need to know where your heart is, as well as the hearts of those you love. That will determine how long your relationship will last. By the way, ask Lot if God is concerned about who you spend the rest of your life with. The thing about a relationship test is God will surprise you out of the blue with a situation from time to time to see who you are most dedicated to. Make sure you pass.

Prayer: Dear Jesus, test us, and show us where we are not totally committed to You. Then, test those who are with us so that we can see what we should do. Then, give us the strength to make the hard decisions. We pray that their hearts, and ours, are sold on obeying You so that we can walk together hand in hand while You guide our next step. In Jesus' name I pray, Amen.

Questions

1. Have you ever chosen someone over God? What was the outcome?

2. How long did you feel comfortable not obeying or living in the Will of God?

3. Do you find yourself being more comfortable living in the past than looking at the future the Lord has for you? Why?

4. What strengths can you focus on that you have learned that will assist you in moving forward with the directive the Lord has planned for you?

"Double Standards"

Proverbs 20:10: "The Lord despises double standards of every kind."

Have you ever been in a situation where you were doing your best to reach the goals that were set before you, but it seemed as if somebody kept changing the rules on you? It seems you get to work earlier, work harder, do other people's work that they get credit for (and they come in late everyday and get a promotion), while you're late one day, and get written up. Does it seem that as a woman you have to work twice as hard as a man at keeping your reputation clean? You go on friendly dates with two different guys - just for dinner, that's it - and you get labeled a loose woman, but a guy can sleep with twelve women, and he's just a man being a man. Does it make sense that a vice president of the United States can shoot a man and nothing happens to him, and an ordinary brother on the streets does the same thing and gets 40 years without parole? Is it right for one president to get impeached for sexual misconduct and then another president gets reelected (or elected for the first time after the first fiasco) after telling lie after lie on videotape about weapons of mass destruction? Does it make sense that Christians in the pews can drink, cuss, smoke, fornicate, club, drive the nicest cars, and there is no problem with them thinking they are okay with God, but a preacher who gets a nice car after praying for the member who got cancer from smoking, the sister who has a fornication attachment to a married man, the mother whose son was shot at the club, and helping the brother who can't stop drinking get into rehab, is not following God? The definition of double standard is, "A set of principles allowing greater opportunity or liberty to one than the other." When it is in the Will of God it is called favor. When it is driven by selfish ambition, and used to oppress others emotionally, spiritually, socially, and economically, it is called a double standard! The Bible sets the tone and the standard of how we should see and treat one another. It sets the tone for how we should live before the eyes of God. If we raise up what we do in comparison to what someone else does, then it may look pretty good. If we raise both up to God then we may find that both of us fall short. Make sure, friend, that you know the true standard is not what we think, but what God thinks about the big picture. When we do that, we will make wiser decisions, love more, and people will begin to be treated as one class instead of upper, middle, and lower. (Those classes are man-made by the way.)

Prayer: Dear Jesus, help us to live, and treat one another as You would have us to treat one another. You are the standard, and we have a long way to go before we get there. Teach us to help, and not hinder one another in the process. In Jesus' name I pray, Amen.

Questions

1. Have you lived a "Double Standard" lifestyle? Why, and what caused you to do this?

2. When you see people living this lifestyle, knowing you lived the same way at one time, are you more empathetic to them? Do you correct them? How?

3. Do you know the true standard that the Lord would like for you live?

4. What things have you changed or do you need to change in order for you to focus on not living a "Double Standard" and living His standards for you?

"Love Never Gives Up"

I Corinthians 13:7: "Love never gives up, never loses faith, is always hopeful, and endures through every circumstance."

"We Sell Gas Now" reads the big red and white sign that hangs outside a gas station not far from my office. This gas station was once frequented by many who would get an occasional refill of their favorite and much needed gasoline so they could go on about their daily and weekly routines. However, one day I drove up in much need of gas, and the station was open, but, to my dismay, none of the gas pumps worked. So, here I am at a gas station trying to get what I really need, but all it had available were snacks on the inside of the store. This particular station has remained opened without selling gas for almost a year. There have been many that had the need I had, and had a similar experience of not getting their need met, but today it has voiced to the world that "We Sell Gas Now!" Essentially, what the station is saying is that it was shut down for repairs, but is fully functional once again. This time when you drive up, you will not be disappointed. That is much like loving people. Sometimes their hearts shut down because of hurts, disappointments, or any other life experiences that caused them to need healing before being useful for full service again. They may be only able to give you snack time and snack conversations during their period of repair. There may be many who came to you while you were not functioning properly, and went away disappointed. Don't despair. Your true customers, your true friends, recognized that you just needed some time to heal. Now that you've had some time to get re-fueled, it's time to put that smile on your face, and put that pep in your step that says, "I'm Ready to Love Again!" Others may have given up on you, but love yourself enough to heal properly so you can be ready for full service again. "Love Never Gives Up", but it does take time to assess damage so it can be ready for future use. Love Never Fails, but people fail at loving. Get up and try again. Never give up!

Prayer: Dear Jesus, thank You for not giving up on me when I have wanted to give up on myself, and so many others. Bless everyone not to give up on receiving or giving love, but take the time to heal in their areas of weakness so that they can be opened to fully love others as You have designed them to do. In Jesus' name I pray, Amen.

Questions

1. When you gave up, did you have a support system to guide you through your process?

2. Did you find yourself withdrawing from the Lord's love along with those who may have hurt you? How did you guide yourself back to Him? If you are still in the process, what are you still focused on in your process?

3. During this time, did you only receive love or only give love, not giving fully either way? Why?

4. Through your continued healing process, what can you do so you will know that His love never fails and you should not give up?

"I Know That's Right!"

Psalm 139:14: "I will praise thee, for I am fearfully and wonderfully made: marvelous are thy works; and that my soul knoweth right well."

By looking at the verse the Psalmist writes above, on the surface one would think this writer was full of himself. Yet, when you get the meaning of a few words, it brings things more into perspective. He begins with praise to God. Then we find the reason why He is thanking God. He is thanking God because God made him fearfully. Fearfully, in the original language, means "with awe; astounding." In essence, he was saying, "God, I am in awe that You would hook me up like this." Then he says, "God made me wonderfully." Wonderfully means "distinct, separated, set apart." The writer was saying here to God, "Man, You didn't make anyone like me, and no one can beat me being me. There is nothing to compare me to because I am unique." He then says God's works are just awesome and marvelous. I really love the last part. He closes by saying, "My soul knoweth right well." Sounds to me like he was thinking about all that God had done for him, and he had nothing to do with who he was, and how he was created. He was thinking about how he doesn't have to compare himself to anyone else because God made only one of him. He was thinking about God taking time to shape his life, his looks, his walk, and every fabric of his internal and external being. He was thinking about the heart God had created him to have, as well as the thought process he possessed. Then he began to feel good about himself because God designed him specifically the way He did for a reason, and that was such a blessing when he came to accept who he was instead of trying to be something he wasn't. He then says to the Lord in my own words, "No matter what others may think or how I may feel about myself, You have hooked me up! I know that's right! I don't have to get validation from other people. I can be short, tall, bald, thin, light, dark, or whatever phase I may go through. Either way Lord, it's all good because You made me good!" Friend, you have to know you are wonderful because God says so. Just because you don't feel like you are because of choices you've made or things you think you should have, you still have it going on! Everything else you get is an accessory! Look in the mirror, and tell the Lord, "I know that's right!" That's not arrogance, but confidence because it was God who made you that way! Now go strut your stuff in Jesus' name!

Prayer: Dear Jesus, forgive me for ever seeking validation in others for what You already approved. Help me accept who You made me to be, whether or not others can appreciate this wonderful package You put together. Thank You for hooking me up. Help me remind others that they have been hooked up by You! In Jesus' name I pray, Amen.

Questions

1. Why have you ever felt like you needed validation from someone besides God?

2. When someone told you something that was contrary to what you viewed in your mind, how did you feel?

3. As the Psalmist said, "I am fearfully and wonderfully made." Can you truthfully express that about yourself no matter what society says?

4. If there are areas you need to focus on in order to state the scripture as a truthful statement for yourself, what are they, and how can you change your mindset without the confirmation from someone?

"Waiting To Exhale"

Luke 23:46: "Then Jesus shouted, 'Father, I entrust my spirit into your hands!' And with those words he breathed his last."

One of the greatest feelings in the world is to be open, and honest with someone. We all want to be able to be free to be who we are, and not have to experience being rejected or being judged. As rough as life is, sometimes you just want to come to a point, to a place, to a person, where you can just open up, and trust them with your spirit. Jesus had been working all these years to help others and meet their needs. While dying on the cross, His last words in Luke are "I entrust My spirit into Your hands." Of course He was talking to His Father who never judged Him, never rejected Him, and always saw Him for who He was. Trust is something most, if not all humans, struggle with. It is refreshing to find a friend or loved one you can trust with your spirit before you take your last breath, and your journey ends on this earth. Like Jesus, we too must go through struggles and hardships in life while trying to do our best at whatever we have been purposed to do. But also like Jesus, when the people near us can't be there for us, we can always turn to the Father, and exhale, and take our rest. And yet, there is another struggle huh? Many people struggle with trusting the Father (God), because we really don't think He cares, or has our best interest in mind because certain things happened or didn't happen that we prayed about. Friend, there is no One you can trust more than God. You can go to Him today, and tell Him all your secrets, struggles, triumphs, and desires. You can be yourself, and it will feel so refreshing that you will feel more uplifted than you've ever been. Stop holding your breath, waiting to find someone you can share with. You've always had a Friend in Jesus. Write Him a letter, sing Him a song, or simply open your mouth in your private time with Him, and EXHALE. When Jesus exhaled, He died, but He rose again in three days. When you exhale you die to your fear and lack of trust, and God can then resurrect your energy and emotions to live life on a greater level. You've done that already? Do it again! He's still the True Answer to all of life's issues. Isn't it time to breathe again?

Prayer: Dear Jesus, help me trust You more and more. Help me learn to talk with You about everything, even the things I think don't concern You. You are my Best Friend, so help me grow in Our relationship. In Jesus' name I pray, Amen.

Questions

1. While going through struggles, and hardships in life, have you ever felt as though you could not trust the Lord, and decided to do things your own way? Why?

2. What caused you to realize that He has your best interest at heart and when?

3. When you were able to "Exhale" again, how did you feel?

4. The next time you feel as though no one is listening, and you need someone to take the pain away, how can you focus your mind on the Lord, and talk to Him about EVERYTHING?

"Who Is The Real Competition?"

1 Samuel 18:8: "Saul was very angry; this refrain galled him. 'They have credited David with tens of thousands,' he thought, 'but me with only thousands. What more can he get but the kingdom?'"

"We're all on the same team!" Has that statement ever come into your mind? Have you ever wanted to shout that out in the middle of a meeting? We Americans are so competitive! Competition has its place: football, basketball, beauty pageants, boat races, dog fights, insurance companies...on and on and on I could go. It's a competitive market, and it very well should be. Should Christians compete? If you work in a worldly system you should. Yet, when it comes to churches, we need to sit down for a moment and think that one over. When it comes to family members, we need to get it in check. When it comes to friends, we need to re-evaluate. Saul asked David to come and serve in his kingdom. David came and worked for Saul with all of his heart. They were like family. David even found his pal for life in Saul's son named Jonathan. The sad tale that we see so often happened next. David did the job he was asked to do so well he began to be noticed. Saul began to be jealous and felt he could not compete with this newcomer, so he tried to kill the competition. That mindset was wrong. David wasn't the competition. David was the confirmation. David's good work should have been confirmation to Saul that he had chosen the right person to help build his kingdom.

The enemy wasn't David. The enemy was what Saul hired David to kill. They had the same enemy, and together could accomplish more when they respected each other's gifts. Instead of praying for David, he began to prey on David. Sad, Sad, Sad! Friend, when someone begins to hate you because of what you were asked to do, they have lost focus on who the real competition is. Does it bother you sometimes to see others do better than you in an area? If you are human it may make you pause and think, but don't think too long. Begin to pray that God blesses them more and more. Then watch God give you new ideas or another assignment that you will grow in because your season is changing. True maturity is celebrating another's success, especially if they achieved it with integrity. If they didn't, pray that they learn integrity and that God blesses their socks off! We're all on the same team, friend, and if they're not on Your team, then you have some decisions to make. Saul forgot that God put him on the throne and only God could take him off. Maybe he finally lost it because he forgot that simple, yet major detail.

Prayer: Dear Jesus, give us a spirit of unity and support on our jobs, in our families, in our churches, and among other entities we have to be a part of throughout our lives. You are so disappointed when we disconnect from one another due to jealousy and strife. That is not Your attitude. Help us join together and combat the real enemy while we grow together in love and strength. In Jesus' name I pray, Amen.

Questions

1. When someone did not support you in your growth at work, church, etc., how did you feel? If this was a team member, did he/she express it verbally or non-verbally?

2. Does it bother you sometimes to see others do better than you in an area? Why?

3. Do you realize that you may have certain gifts and others may have the other portion of the gift in order to assist you or the team succeed? Has this occurred before?

4. How can you focus on becoming a better team player and/or assist someone else in doing so?

"Family Problems/ Family Solutions"

Genesis 45:3: "'I am Joseph!' he said to his brothers. 'Is my father still alive?' But his brothers were speechless! They were stunned to realize that Joseph was standing there in front of them."

Why did Joseph have to tell his own brothers who he was? They didn't recognize him because it had been so long since they had really seen him. Actually, they didn't recognize him even when he was younger because they tried to kill him. The first time they didn't recognize who he was on the inside, they mishandled him. Later in life they didn't recognize who he was on the outside because they had not been on speaking terms in so long, they thought he was dead. But Joseph shouts, "I am Joseph!" He probably was waiting to tell his brothers this because even after all they had done, he was the mature one who was taking care of them in the present because he forgave them for what they tried to do to him in his past. Every family will have problems they face in life. Every family! Many of them never get around to solutions because they spend so much time blaming rather than forgiving. Being hurt and abused are things that run deep when they are caused by the hands and the mouths of those who were supposed to love and protect you, support and provide for you. But it doesn't always work out that way, does it? You know the answer to that one. It had been years, and Joseph surely lived with what he would say once he finally got a chance to see his family again after all they had done years before. He trips a little at first by playing games because they needed him. But after he gets through that, he tells them, "I am Joseph!" I am not the little boy you tried to kill years ago. I have grown up now. That means I recognize that humans do dumb things sometimes. Life isn't fair, but God has worked it all out for my good. Even what you did to me made me a stronger person. So with that, I'm going to love you, forgive you, and take care of you because you are family. Wow! So you don't think you can do what Joseph did yet, huh? It just means you have to grow in God like Joseph did so you can stop blaming and start building your life and that of your family again. Still having problems? Just think of what God really should do after all the times you left Him, disappointed Him, and totally broke His heart over and over again. If He can forgive, restore, and provide for you as His child after your mess, who are you not to forgive, love, and pray for those in your family? Challenging I know, but is the story of Joseph a reflection of what God desires of us and our family after or during a struggle?

Prayer: Dear Jesus, I pray that You give me the ability to look at my family through Your eyes rather than my own. Your eyes have forgiveness when mine have anger, resentment, and even hatred at times. Please help me to look at my family like You look at me - with love in spite of all I have done. In Jesus' name I pray, Amen.

Questions

1. Do you feel as though your family is no longer a team or has never been a team? Why?

2. How do you handle family conflicts? Would or have you handled a work problem the same way with your family? Why or why not?

3. You must use wisdom. List all your options when issues arise so you can be more objective.

4. It's okay to express how you feel as Joseph did. But make sure they know you love them in the midst of the situation. People tend to feel they can weather almost any crisis when they are loved. How can you focus on telling or showing them you love them though you may have been treated like Joseph?

"Your Wedding Day Could Be Sooner Than You Think!"

Isaiah 62:4: "No more will anyone call you Rejected and your country will no more be called Ruined. You'll be called Hephzibah (My Delight), and your land Beulah (Married), because God delights in you and your land will be like a wedding celebration." (The Message Translation)

Many people long to see the day when they will finally have the "Right" person in their lives. Others just want a body to take to the altar that is half of everything they prayed for because they spend more time preparing for a wedding than they do for a marriage. Whether you have been married and are single again, whether you are single and have never been married, whether you are married and it doesn't feel like it any longer, I have some great news for you. Isaiah is praying for Jerusalem and begins to prophesy about her future. He looks at her current condition and realizes that she has been rejected and seemingly forsaken by God, although God still loves Israel very much. Have you ever felt like that? Israel longed for communion, the feeling of love and protection, having her needs met. Yet, she kept searching for it and was unsuccessful. Isaiah says things are about to change for Israel in the future. You have to read all of Chapter 62 for the whole story, but in essence, Israel was about to get married. She would have a new name, but the name would come from God Himself. That is point number 1: Don't take or give away a name unless that name has been approved by God. Her new name would be My Delight, or God's Delight! Point number 2 is simply this: Go where you are celebrated and not tolerated. Read Verse 3 for a wonderful expression of celebration of someone you are going to marry. The last thing about this wedding that will lead to a wonderful marriage is found in the next part of the verse. "No more will anyone call you Rejected, and your country will no longer be called Ruined." You may feel rejected and actually be rejected in certain ways even if you are married. Point number 3 is simply this: Even when you feel rejected by a man or a woman, know that God will never reject you. Therefore, there is never a need to feel insecure about your relationship from His side. Friend, although this passage, in context, is speaking of the day when Christ returns and marries the church, the principles are the same for when you get married on earth. It must be done God's way with His approval. You should feel acceptance, you should feel celebrated, and not feel as though you are a burden. Make sure you are engaged to Jesus before you try to get married to anyone else. First thing's first. Hook up with Jesus and treat Him like He should be treated on a day-to-day basis and your wedding day may be much closer than you think because He has a way of giving you things when He sees you are mature enough to handle them...even if it is your second time around. No longer shall you be called Rejected or Ruined, but you shall be called Beulah (Married). That promise to Israel came with conditions. So does your promise for God to give you the desires of your heart. The conditions are to know where the blessing will come from and follow directions. Do you believe that? Then start getting ready for a marriage and Jesus will take care of the Wedding in His own time if this Word is connecting with your spirit!

Prayer: Dear Jesus, help us not to live our life just for a wedding date, but help us live our lives preparing for the marriage we will have with You. As we travel through this life, if You desire for us to be married to a man or a woman, help us to recognize that if You decide to bless us in that way, we should already have our focus on our relationship with You first and never lose focus of it at anytime, even if You bless us with someone. If they reject us we can still feel valuable because we are a delight in Your eyes. In Jesus' name I pray, Amen.

Questions

1. Do you currently or did you in past relationships feel as though you were forsaken by God? Why or why not?

2. Have you ever felt insecure about your relationship with God?

3. If you are single: In what areas do you feel you need to grow in your own life before you get married? If you are married: What can you do to enhance the marriage the Lord has granted?

4. How can you focus on your relationship with God first and never lose focus on it while waiting on your mate or while in your marriage?

"How's Your Love Life?"

John 15:12-13 "My command is this: Love each other as I have loved you. Greater love has no one than this, that he lay down his life for his friends."

February has been given the label "Black History Month." As I sat in a hotel in downtown New Orleans 18 months after Hurricane Katrina, as I walked through the poorest sections of New Orleans in the 9th Ward and other areas which still look like a hurricane just hit it yesterday, and I recognized the skin color of those who were helping to rebuild the thousands of houses that were destroyed in mostly black neighborhoods were about 80 percent non-African American. I walked in and drove by several of the black churches that were destroyed by flood waters. I talked with a 24-year old brother who had a tie on and was looking for a job on the River Walk. As I continued walking, I came upon another brother on the street in his twenties looking for a job, and we dialogued. I must say I had to change the name of this month someone called Black History Month. As I looked at teenage girl after teenage girl roll around baby after baby, not in school because the schools in the 9th Ward were not up and running, as I saw my black people, ones who were actually trying to do something with their lives, but had no jobs, no homes, and seemingly no hope, I had to change the name of this month someone called Black History Month. The new name for this month is Black Mystery Month! I know the government didn't and hadn't shown us much love, but why are we not loving each other as we should? I mean, after all we have been through as a people, do we really no longer know what love really is? Although poverty exists in every city, although all cultures struggle with these issues, I, being African-American, must question if we are living up to Christ's command, not suggestion, to "Love Each Other as He Loved Us." Should you enjoy your fine home and nice job? If you put the work in, you should enjoy all that you worked hard to get? Should you enjoy your kids being able to go to private schools to get a better education? You should put them in the best school your money can buy. Should you eat fine, drive first class vehicles, and dress fly? Do your thang, my brother, my sistah! But all of that is loving yourself. That's good love, but you have not even begun to love like Christ. "Greater love has no one than this that he lay down his life for his friends." If you are so busy that you don't make time to love someone else enough to help them get their house, help them get their children a good education, help someone else have proper clothing and food, then you are failing miserably at love. "Love each other as I have loved you." Christ wants us to love all cultures. Even He, being a Jew, went to His own first. I see this pain and try to help on a daily basis wherever I may go. Yet, I had to repent that week because my love life had been more focused on me than others even in my best attempts. I can do better. So, how is your love life, friend? If there are homeless people, hungry people, and helpless people who could do better, and desire to do better within 10 miles of you, then you can do better if it is in your power to help and you do nothing. Do you really want to have a Happy Valentines Day? While looking forward to receiving a pair of shoes, give a pair away. While looking forward to having a nice dinner, make sure someone gets to eat who hasn't eaten. And if you are single and don't have a Valentine, you still have someone to show some love to. Being your race and showing love are year-round goals, not month-long. Lay down your life (agenda) a little bit more to love someone like Christ has loved you...through all your issues, to bring you to where you are. If you have a problem with this that means you are still too selfish. I will pray for you to learn to share all you have that God is allowing you to borrow while you live on His earth.

Prayer: Dear Jesus, please forgive me where I have failed to love Your children because I have been more concerned about someone loving me. Please forgive me for not sharing or making time to share with others who are less fortunate than me. Forgive me for judging someone else and not knowing the situation. Thank You for reminding me that You have shown and continue to show me love and that if you ever stopped I would be in very pitiful condition. Help me love more like You. In Jesus' name I pray, Amen.

Questions

1. When was the last time you showed love to someone you did not know? If you haven't, why not?

2. Do you find yourself loving yourself when you could be loving others more? Example: If you have a day off would you use some of your time off to volunteer?

3. In this time in your life, is the focus more on you and your family's needs and wants? What would happen if you needed assistance and no one was there?

4. What actions can you take to carve time out of your schedule so you can help those who are less fortunate than you, like Christ did?

"Is It Better To Marry Than To Burn?"

1 Corinthians 7:9 "But if they can't control themselves, they should go ahead and marry. It's better to marry than to burn with lust."

"If you can't keep your zipper zipped then you need to go ahead and get married!" "Why buy the cow when you can get the milk for free?" Have you ever heard or said either of these things? If so, the first statement was said about a man who was struggling with sex or the idea of sex while trying to be a Christian and live right. They were told to go ahead and marry someone because they just had to have sex. So get married and your lust will go away, right? The second statement was said to or about a woman who had concerned people in her life, and were trying to help her keep herself pure by comparing her to an animal who had a valuable part of itself taken from away by someone with no interest in buying the whole cow. I'm sure you've heard these, right? There are two problems here. First, many men got married only to recognize that a ring doesn't control lust. Second, their marriages suffered the consequences because of sexual addictions, pornography, and extra-marital affairs. And must I say the same things happened to women. The women and the cow analogy doesn't work because cows don't willingly offer their milk. It's taken from them the last time I checked out the milking process. And by the way, why would you want to be compared to a fat, boring animal in the first place? So what does Paul mean when he says, "It's better to marry than to burn?" The scripture starts off saying, "But if they can't control themselves." If you can't control yourself before marriage, why would you think you could once you got married? What is lack of control you may ask? Can you stop masturbating although you aren't having sex with another person? Can you stop looking at pornography, going to strip clubs, viewing those freaky e-mails and magazines, using sex toys while you are single? Did these things carry over into your marriage? I know. Your mouth is wide open, huh? Friend, that's reality for a lot of people, Christian people, in the world today. What the Word of God says is exercise self-control. So you must learn to control yourself and not make excuses or justify what you are comfortable doing because you don't see it point blank in the Bible. If these things are a struggle for you, your answer is not necessarily marriage to the first person you meet. It is learning to control yourself the best way you can, asking for God's strength and grace as you grow in this area, waiting until you build a healthy, growing, mature relationship with someone, and not just marrying someone because you want to have sex. It's better to control yourself. If you are struggling with someone you have been shacking with for the last few years, and you plan on being together, you need to go ahead and make it legal...with proper guidance, of course. In that case, it is better to marry than to burn with lust. Fight the good fight, friend. Marriage is too important to jump into just to jump into bed. Ask God for strength in your weakness and set boundaries for yourself. It's a fight, but wake up everyday willing to fight again! Your future depends on it. Don't let your weakness pressure you to make a long term decision to which you're not ready to commit. Don't let well meaning married people pressure you to get married because you have sexual urges. God gave you the urge. You must control it and release it at the proper time. Challenge? I know! Wait on God. One reason the divorce rate is higher is because of this poor advice from people who have been married longer than they have been single. It is better to be in the will of God and fight to stay holy than to burn with regret, anger, pain, and see your kids go through hell because you married the wrong person for the wrong reason. Forgive yourself, get back up, and grow one step closer to God today, friend! You have a bright future ahead of you and God will help you every step of the way. Now, for those of you who don't struggle, but just think all of the above is OK because God wants you to be happy and He knows your heart, God wants us to be HOLY! Happiness is not always connected to that, but we are better off in the long run. And your heart needs to be healed and made sensitive to the Spirit of God. Fight, friend! Fight with prayer, boundaries, and letting go of some things, people, and situations that feel good, but lead you to do bad things. Getting counseling doesn't make you crazy, it makes you care.

Prayer: Dear Jesus, I pray that You penetrate the hearts of every person who struggles with lust. Help those who are in denial, help those who are out of control, and help those who judge those who have a struggle to begin to pray rather than point fingers. You have saved all of us by Your grace, so heal marriages that suffer and singles who struggle. We want to be real with You and whole within ourselves to be pure before You. In Jesus' name I pray, Amen.

Questions

1. Why do we let our weaknesses pressure us into making a long term decisions to which we are not ready to commit?

2. Do we allow our weakness of loneliness and society to persuade us of having sex alone or with someone?

3. What are your struggles when it comes to living a life without burning? Single: having sex before marriage? Married: having sex outside of our marriage or being selfish with our sexual activity?

4. How can you focus on staying pure until your mate comes into your life or in your marriage?

"Don't Get Used To It!"

John 5:6 "When Jesus saw him and knew he had been ill for a long time, He asked him, "Would you like to get well?"

As I was driving I looked up at a sign for gas and saw the price was $3.23. This gas station was one of the cheaper stations on the strip I was on. One could look at that and say, "That's a low price!" The reality is, prices were a dollar cheaper a few years ago. In order to raise gas prices, and keep them high, the government raised the prices very high, and left them high for a while. We complained, vowed protest, and soon became weary of fighting. They were trying to get us used to paying a higher price for gas because it was something we desired, and many needed. In order to make us get used to the higher prices, they would drop the prices a few pennies from time to time. Since they got us used to higher prices, a few pennies seemed like a discount! We had forgotten what good prices were, and had gotten so used to being robbed that we began to appreciate being not robbed of as much! This man in our text Jesus was speaking of had been lame for 38 years. Maybe he once walked, and then got so used to not walking that he just adjusted to his condition. He adjusted so much so that Jesus had to remind him he actually could walk around, and did not have to settle for lying around. Friend, don't get so used to people who treat you less than what you are. Don't get comfortable not having enough money at the end of the month. Don't get accustom to settling for a relationship that is beneath your standards because you feel what you desire or deserve is nowhere in view. Don't adapt to being labeled as a statistic! If you never have experienced anything good or better, know that there is something better. If this person beats you, but doesn't beat you as much as the last person and you stay in the relationship, know that you are still being beaten! If he/she cheats, but not as much as the last person, know that he/she still cheats! If you're disrespected, but not as much as the last time, you're still disrespected! If a leader lies, but not as much as the last one, the leader still lies! Accepting anything less than what you are and not fighting for more makes you a content slave. Free yourself! Jesus is asking you a question: "Would you like to be made well?" Would you like to get more than what you have gotten accustom to because you have given up hope for anything better? If you answer, "Yes," then you are required to believe there is more and ask Jesus to give you strength to position yourself for more. If you answer, "No," then be content in your slavery and blame no one but yourself for being where you are. Don't settle for lesser treatment or a lesser level of life, friend! There's a better way! There really is. Aren't you anxious to see it?

Prayer: Dear Jesus, we do want to be made well. Help us see where we have settled and give us strength to adjust our expectations to Your expectations for us. In Jesus' name I pray, Amen.

Questions

1. Have you found yourself settling in a situation because you did not know anything better?

2. Have you settled knowing that you could change your situation? Why did you settle?

3. Do those around you assist you in focusing on your goals and changing your surroundings? If not, why? Are they enabling you?

4. How can you focus on getting up, not settling, and gaining strength to adjust your expectations and not what others may expect from you?

"Make The Right Choice"

Jeremiah 29:11 "'For I know the plans I have for you,' says the Lord. 'They are plans for good and not disaster, to give you a future and a hope.'"

If you look at all of the decisions you have made in your past, I'm sure you can find several that you wish you could change. You can look back at those decisions and ask yourself the question, "What was I thinking?" Ever done that? Our decisions reflect our character. In essence, we choose based on our beliefs about what we are choosing and how it will benefit us in the process at that point in our lives. Maturity brings about different and better choices. We think we know what's best for us without consulting God and waiting on His answers. Many times we choose based on what we would like to see rather than what is reality. Self-deception has made many a man and woman make poor choices. Jeremiah tells us that God has plans to prosper us that will give us hope and a positive future. So what went wrong in our hopeless, negative past? We either did not have the character we needed in those areas or we were deceived. There's a proverb that states, "The slower you go the sooner you arrive." That simply means it is easier to see problems, analyze benefits, and think through consequences of a choice before you make it when you are not rushed and anxious. Patience brings about better choices. So the slower you go, the sooner you are able to enjoy what you really desired rather than having to come back and clean up things you could have prevented that cost you extra time.

In order for you to get God's perfect plan and minimize disaster, you must make the right choices. Continue this year by making a decision to tell yourself the truth, not live in an illusion of what you want to see, but what is reality and face it. Then ask God to direct your steps so every choice you make will be better than the ones you have made in the past. Why? Your peace of mind depends on it!

Prayer: Dear Jesus, the best choice I have ever made was to be in relationship with You. I need to make more choices like that in my life, so show me the value in whatever I may attempt to choose. Show me whether it will help me or hinder me from doing what You designed me to do in my life. Thank You for being the Director of my Life, and help me listen more to You this year. In Jesus' name I pray, Amen.

Questions

1. What decisions have you made in your past that you now wish you had been more mature in order to have made the better choices?

2. Describe your character. Describe what others say about your character. Now, what does the Lord say your character should reflect or be?

3. Did the decisions you listed for Question 1 strain your relationship(s) with the Lord and/or those around you? How?

4. What will help you focus on those things that the Lord has designed for your life rather than the things that are hindrances to you?

"Runaway Love"

Hosea 2:7 "When she runs after her lovers she won't be able to catch them. She will search for them and then not find them. Then she will think, "I might as well return to my husband for I was better off with him than I am now."

Many people say they want love, but really don't know how to accept true, genuine, authentic love. Their only concept of love is when there is so much dysfunction involved. They see someone trying to love them without drama as untrustworthy because they never really had pure love displayed to them. Gomer, the wife of Hosea, had that same problem. Israel, the Children of God, were in that boat as well. Gomer and Israel both had a good thing, but didn't know how to handle it. Gomer had a God-fearing man who was faithful and loved the kids. Yet, her past was one of men only wanting her for her body. She would use her body to survive and have sex and suppress her feelings so she wouldn't have any intimacy because maybe no man ever really loved her for who she really was without drama. Israel had God Himself loving her. She didn't want for anything. Still, both of them ran away from their good situation. Why? When you have been living, loving, and being broken for so long, you begin to feel like there will never be someone who will love you just as you are. You begin to do crazy things and say crazy things in order to push people away because of the fear of being hurt or rejected. Then these feelings, thoughts and actions become stronger than your desire to really enjoy something that feels so good and seemingly what you need in your life. You sabotage a good thing because you get the mindset that all people are alike, or you just don't feel you deserve the love you are receiving because of where you have been in your life. Either way, when Israel ran away from God and chased after her old lifestyle of taking up every man's offer that came her way while she was still in relationship with God, God just let her get it out of her system, but limited what she could do. Then she came to her senses. When she got tired of running, when she saw that the way she used to live was still empty because she now had been exposed to a real man who didn't play games with her, she decided to go back home. God told Hosea to buy back his cheating wife! Friend, loving people through their brokenness is not an easy task at all. God used the term "husband" as it relates to His relationship with Israel. He didn't divorce Israel because He got into the relationship knowing the issues upfront and gave Israel time to work through those issues, and come to her senses. Broken people run from genuine love sometimes. How long did you run from doing what God wanted you to do? How long did it take for you to get saved? See what I mean? Trust someone again, friend. Don't run. If you can't trust them, then trust God and He will never leave you nor forsake you. You don't have to run any longer. It's time to accept love again…real love.

Prayer: Dear Jesus, thank You for loving me and being patient every time I have run from Your will and Your love. Thank You for not giving up on me when I was afraid and fearful of something that looked too genuine to be true. Thank You for loving the fear out of me and showing me what true love really is, that it doesn't have to be full of games and drama. Help me and those who read this to only commit to a love like Yours with no games or gimmicks; a love full of forgiveness and patience. Help us grow up and into what You desire us to be. In Jesus' name I pray, Amen.

Questions

1. Have you done crazy things in order to push people away because of the fear of being hurt or rejected due to past situations? Why?

2. Do you have the mindset that all people are alike? Why? Is this relative to all people or only people from certain settings? (Example: co-workers, family, church, etc.)

3. How long did you run from doing what God wanted you to do or accepting His love?

4. How can you focus on His love so you can recognize when to only commit to real love without games or gimmicks, a love full of forgiveness and patience?

"Could He Pastor Your Church?"

Ephesians 5:23 "For the husband is the head of the wife as Christ is the head of the church, his body, of which he is the savior."

I remember talking and praying to God about the person with whom I would share my life. While I was waiting on an answer of who, and still am, God began to talk to me about church! I was like, "Did You not hear what I was praying about?" Then I began to think of the verse for today. If I am going to be a husband one day, I must understand some things about Christ and His relationship with His bride-to-be...the Church. I began to reflect on how many people treat the church. Many treat their husbands or husbands-to-be like the people treat church. How is that? They show up and may not commit for years at a time. They just visit. They come looking to see if they can get their needs met. They want to know if they will be fed. They expect the pastor to do his best and meet their needs, yet they don't give anything to the offering. If they do give to the offering, many then think since they have given they have the right now to control what goes on in the church. They don't give because it's right to give; they give because it gets them something in return. When they don't like decisions that are made, they stop giving, yet still show up, and won't give again until they feel like it. Then, many can't stay at one church. They go from church to church looking for the perfect pastor. They feel this one didn't meet their needs so they keep searching and searching and won't get stable and allow their relationship to grow because something always just isn't right. Another thing about certain churches is many don't want a pastor, but a preacher. Most people today stay at a church only 2 to 3 years. Most marriages last only 2 to 3 years. Strange, huh? A pastor will lead you, guide you, make decisions, and feed your soul. Some churches just want the pastor to preach and that's it. The church people will handle the money, and tell people what to do. You just give them what they need, and make me feel good when I need you. Then I thought to myself, "Man, I need to find the right "church!" No "church" is perfect, but I need one that wants to be led, and wants to commit, and give, and love unconditionally. I need a "church" that wants to grow, and let me use my gifts!" Lady, could a man pastor your "church?" I know what you are saying, "It depends on the kind of "pastor" he is!" That is what this devotional is concerning. This is about you. Will you support your "pastor", love your "pastor" unconditionally, pray for your "pastor", commit to your "pastor", and not leave your "pastor" when he makes mistakes? Or will you leave and find another one because you are not getting fed? Many times people leave their "churches" because they have not learned to feed themselves! We're waiting on someone else to give us what we should have learned to do ourselves. That's maturity, which brings stability. Married lady, what kind of "church" are you? Single lady, do you want a "preacher" or a "pastor?" Right now you may have an interim. Determine whether or not you want to hire him or fire him because you will be expected to grow with and follow him if you choose him…just as he is!

Prayer: Dear Jesus, I pray that You help those to be the church You desire for them to be to You. Let Your relationship with us be carefully looked at before we try to be in relationship with someone else. Help us to be what we and You are desiring to have in our lives. In Jesus' name I pray, Amen.

Questions

1. Have you carefully looked at your relationship with the Lord before trying to enter into a relationship with someone else? What do you need to change?

2. Ladies: When you think of someone being the "pastor" of your "church", what do you envision? Men: When you envision being the "pastor" of your "church", what do you see?

3. Married Lady: What kind of church are you? Single Lady: Do you want a "preacher" or a "pastor"? Men: Are you a "preacher" or a "pastor"?

4. What can you do so your focus is on the Lord and becoming mature enough to handle the "church" that is being built or the "pastor" who is to receive His Word?

"Is He The Right Pastor For Your Church?"

Ephesians 5:23 "For the husband is the head of the wife as Christ is the head of the church..."

Once again, while looking and meditating on male/female relationships, God began to point me to Christ's relationship to the church. Christ is the Pastor and Leader of the church. Lady, when a pastor is being interviewed for a church there are several questions that are raised:

1. Are you saved? If so tell me about your salvation experience.

2. Do you feel God is calling you to pastor this church or are you just applying because it is available?

3. Do you have vision that can lead this church to do greater things for God?

4. Do you respect the fact that this church had a vision before you came along, and are you willing to listen and help fulfill that God-given vision while the church grows with the vision God is bringing through you?

5. Do you plan to commit to this church 100 percent, spend quality time, protect, not embarrass, and be faithful to this church?

Friend, before you accept your "pastor", make sure you ask

these questions and many more seeing that he is going to be the one you choose to lead your life. Otherwise, you may accept someone who is not qualified for the job! Look over their resumes carefully. Do some background checks (friends). Look at some references (the family). This job is too serious to end up with a wolf in sheep's clothing! If you don't want to do ministry or impact your life and the lives of others, then a warm body to fill a position of a "lay man" that can preach okay, I guess will do for you. Haven't you had enough of that?

Prayer: Dear Jesus, challenge Your daughters to not choose leaders in their lives who are underqualified and are okay with that. Challenge them to be patient until You reveal the right "pastor" for their church. Help them to be a "church" that doesn't just look and sound good, but one that goes and does good! In Jesus' name I pray, Amen.

Questions

1. Out of the 5 questions asked in the devotional, which one do you feel is the most important one to you? Why?

2. Single Lady: When you think of a "pastor" for your "church" what are your qualifications? Married Lady: Is your husband being a "pastor" to you and your family? How or why not?

3. Before you accept him to be your "pastor" what do you feel needs to be accomplished to ensure he is the right "pastor" for your "church".

4. If you are the "pastor" or the "church" what can you do in order to focus and understand the roles and responsibilities the Lord set in your life so you may be the best person for this position in someone's life?

"Are You Sure You Can Handle It?"

1 Kings 11:4 "As Solomon grew old, his wives turned his heart after other gods, and his heart was not fully devoted to the Lord his God, as the heart of David his father had been."

How could the wisest man to ever live make one of the dumbest choices one could ever make? The same way you and I have made some dumb choices. The choice he made was thinking he could handle something God said he could not. God told Solomon that he should not marry women who were not godly in their thinking, actions, and lifestyle. If he did, the women would turn his heart away from being devoted to God like it needed to be. We all have a little Solomon in us. We think that because we have experience, because we know how to handle situations like this, because we have even helped other people through things, we will recognize things that could potentially cause us harm, right? Not always, my friend. I can imagine Solomon hearing what God said about what these women would do to his relationship with Him, but Solomon took it as a challenge to see how he could step up his wisdom game because he desired to have these women no matter what God said. The text even said, "Solomon held fast to them in love." How many times have we chosen something or someone after being warned because we had become attached to it? Once you are attached, you become vulnerable and it now has an influence in your life. That is why God says, "Guard your heart." You can't let everything or everyone get close to your heart. At the beginning of the relationship, Solomon had control and stood firm on his values and beliefs. As time went by, the pressure began to steer his heart in another direction. Is that how you feel since you have been working on that job you just had to have because you are making money like you never have before? The devil doesn't always kill you right away, friend. He knows how strong you are. All he needs, sometimes, is a little more time. He weakens the strong day by day until one day you wake up so far from who you really are that you wish you had listened to that small, seemingly unimportant feeling in your gut, that lack of peace in your spirit, from day one. Solomon had some good times with what he chose for several years, yet he was disgraced and lost all he had when he grew older because he really began to see the consequences of his bad choice later in life. Although God was displeased with Solomon's decisions in life and with him, He still loved Solomon. Friend, if it's not right, don't try to make it right. Look at it, listen to God, and don't choose whatever it is you are thinking about choosing based on what it looks or feels like now. God can see further down the road than you. He knows whether it will build you or kill you in the long run. Some fights aren't worth fighting. Walk away because there is something better that God has for you that will help you live and die with honor, dignity, and peace. No, you can't handle everything. You aren't that smart or that strong. Be wise and trust God. Then you will become wiser than you have ever been.

Prayer: Dear Jesus, give me a listening ear and a humble heart to not depend on what I think I can do, but help me hear from You on what I should do. Give me discernment and then give me strength to walk away from things that will lead me down the wrong roads of life. I trust You, so keep me close to You so I will only have in my life that which comes from You. In Jesus' name I pray, Amen.

Questions

1. Have any relationships you have entered into made you turn your heart away from God or made your relationship waver with Him? Why?

2. How many times have you chosen something or someone after being warned because you had become attached to it?

3. What was the result of you making these decisions and would you do it again? Looking back, what would you have done differently?

4. When thinking back over the choices you made, what can you focus on that will continue to give you strength to walk away from things that will lead you down the wrong roads in life?

"Relationship Attacks" (Part 1)

Mark 3:25 "If a house is divided against itself, that house cannot stand."

I remember playing sports while growing up and the coaches were always harping on the importance of team unity. Many times the opposing teams were not as good as us, but against some teams, we would end up losing. It wasn't because we were not talented and hadn't practiced hard. It wasn't because we didn't want to win. It was because sometime during the game, someone on my team made a mistake that put us in a bad situation. It wasn't like he meant to do it. It happened because he did not do what he had learned in practice the way he practiced it. We had practiced it over and over again, knew what to do, but did not execute appropriately. How teammates responded determined how we moved forward from that point in the game. If we began to focus on that one incident too long we began to play poorly and lose focus. If we dealt with the issue and moved on to the next play, recognizing that the game wasn't over, we would somehow bounce back and have a better shot at getting back in position to win the game. The key was not getting divided, but staying unified, even if a choice someone made hurt the team. We were still on the same team regardless of what took place. Satan wants people to attack one another when someone in a relationship makes a bad decision in words he uses or actions she takes. The focus now becomes more about what happened, so you stop thinking about the clock and fail to recognize that if you don't pull it together and work through it, your time will run out. Satan hates healthy relationships. If he can't defeat you from the outside he will give you an issue to fight over like not paying money back or feeling like you are not being valued, by not saying anything and acting differently when your feelings are hurt, and many more things. One or both individuals begin(s) to focus on the offense and lose sight of all the good things that happened before it took place. Don't fall for that trick, friend. Relationships are destroyed from the inside out when Satan can't kill them from the outside in. Remember, you are on a team and the enemy is not your teammate, but the enemy is the one who is on the other team. If your enemy is your teammate you may need to switch teams. Usually that is not the case. You can't always run to another family so you need to learn how to get along in that situation. Someone has to be the mature one, right? There's a game on the line. Don't spend so much time dealing with a broken play and pointing out why it went wrong. Encourage, forgive, and support your teammate because when you make a bad play you will need that same support. Now go win the game! You are stronger together than divided in most cases.

Prayer: Dear Jesus, help me to focus on the game and work through broken plays whether I made them or someone on my team did. Every day You model this in Your relationship with me, so help me model those actions in my relationship with others. Help us stand strong and not be divided. In Jesus' name I pray, Amen.

Questions

1. When someone you loved made a mistake and did not mean to do it, although you were upset, how were you able to stay unified and not divide yourself from that person? If there was a division, why?

2. In the situation described above, did you have to divide permanently or temporary? Why? Did you lose full trust in this person? Why or why not?

3. Do you find yourself not being able to forgive someone that has wronged you? Why? If the person had your best interest in mind, (being a team player) would you still focus on his/her "wrong" decision or focus on the good he/she was trying to do?

4. How can you learn to focus on working through and learning from your team's issues, whether you made them or someone on your team did?

"Relationship Attacks" (Part 2)

Galatians 2:11 "But when Peter came to Antioch, I had to oppose him to his face, for what he did was very wrong."

Being a hypocrite is one of the fastest ways to hinder a growing relationship. In our text, Paul explains what hypocrisy is and has to confront Peter about displaying this behavior. Peter was a believer that you are and can be saved by the grace of God and keeping the law. Yet, when people he wanted to please or those who he desired to like him showed up, he began to act funny, and act as if he believed what they believed in order to fit in. Paul recognized that Peter was saying one thing, but doing another. He only stood on what he believed in when it didn't cost him anything. Believe what you believe, and stand on it! Be who you really are at all times. That means don't change how you are with one group of people so another group will like you. You can never please everyone. You can please God by showing integrity of character, though. If you see hypocrisy in a relationship, address it so that the other individual can be helped, but be careful. Many times you may find that they can point out the same behavior in you!

Prayer: Dear Jesus, help us to not be hypocritical, but be who You made us so we can have better relationships! Help me to be who You called me to be so they can see the real me. Help me to conform to Your ways and not earthly ways so they can see You when they see me. In Jesus' name I pray, Amen.

Questions

1. Do you find that you have to conform and cannot be yourself in order to be accepted in your relationship? Why?

2. When you conform, do you compromise your beliefs or standards? Why?

3. When you see others being hypocrites, do you confront them? Why or why not?

4. How can you focus on not being a hypocrite, but be who the Lord made you to be so you can have better relationships, and be a better reflection of Him?

"Relationship Attacks" (Part 3)

Romans 8:35 "Can anything ever separate us from Christ's love? Does it mean he no longer loves us if we have calamity, or are persecuted, or hungry, or destitute, or in danger, or threatened with death?"

One of the greatest tests of a relationship is trouble. You never really know who will stand with you or walk away until you hit some trouble spots in your life or relationship journey. Paul is letting us know that, in this life, all kinds of trouble will come. Some of it we cause ourselves, while other trouble is just part of living. Many times we disconnect from people when it gets too heated for us because we don't like dealing with drama. I feel you deeply on that one. However, the text says that nothing can separate us from the love of God. As a matter of fact, real love isn't real love until it has gone through some real trouble. Trouble shows how sturdy you are, how good your word is, and how much your talk lines up with your walk. Drama is what we least want in our lives. Yet, when you are loving someone, make sure your standard is not the one you set, but the one Christ has set. That standard is very high. Would you want someone to leave you when you were having challenges, even if you were the cause of them? Sometimes, that's what's best, but most times what is best is to work through the challenges to strengthen the love in the relationship. Use wisdom and discernment because anything worth having is worth being tested. Are you loving like Christ or are you loving in a way that is just comfortable for you?

Prayer: Dear Jesus, teach us how to love like You. It takes a lot so help us get there! Help to be sturdy and not waver or separate our love towards You or others when challenges come. In Jesus' name I pray, Amen.

Questions

1. Have you caused trouble in your relationships in order to test the love or commitment of others? Why?

2. Would you want someone to leave you when you were having challenges, even if you were the cause of them? Why?

3. Are you loving like Christ or are you loving in a way that is only comfortable for you? Why?

4. How can you focus on actions and reactions in your relationships when there is a storm? Are you a fair weather friend?

"Don't Miss Your Isaac"

Genesis 24:8 "And if the woman is not willing to follow you, then you will be released from this oath, only do not take my son back there."

Many men and women desire to have the marriage mate that was desired by God for them. Yet, many times that process is hindered because of a character flaw that can be deadly for them in every area of their lives. Abraham wanted a wife for his son Isaac. He sent his servant to find this wife at a specific time, and in a specific place. After his servant found someone who was pleasing, he then told her to follow him. Abraham had given specific instructions to his servant that, "If the girl can't follow your leadership then she won't be able to follow Isaac's. Leave her where she is because she ain't ready!" Rebekah would have missed her man because she did not follow the servant of Abraham who was the servant of the Lord. How well do you follow the current people in your life? How well do you follow your boss, pastor, and other individuals in leadership roles in your life? Rebekah teaches us that if you don't learn to trust people, then you may miss out on why they were in your life in the first place. The servant was the link between her single status and her marital status. Her obedience and submission to his leadership was the order of the day for her to get a desire fulfilled that she may have dreamed of for years. Could it be you have missed your "Isaac" because you did not trust His father's servant sent to test you and lead you to him? Always be found with a humble heart and willing spirit. You never know who God is sending to you to hook you up. If you can't follow or trust them, you're not qualified for your "Isaac" yet. "Isaac" may be a job, relationship, or anything that you desire next in your life. Someone you meet today may be that servant that's linked between your lack and your fullness. Are you willing to trust and follow?

Prayer: Dear Jesus, I know people can be hard to trust, but You aren't. Give us discernment and a willing spirit so that we won't miss our "Isaac" in whatever form that may be. In Jesus' name I pray, Amen.

Questions

1. Do you find it hard to follow specific instructions by the Lord? Why?

2. How well do you follow the current people in your life? Do you have issues following them? Why?

3. Are you willing to follow the person that the Lord has sent into your life? Why or why not?

4. What area/areas in your life must you focus on in order to be a better listener and follower of instructions from the Lord or by someone He has placed in your life?

"God Must Be Crazy!"

Hosea 3:1 "Then the Lord said to me, 'Go and love your wife again, even though she commits adultery with another lover. This will illustrate that the Lord still loves Israel, even though the people have turned to other gods and love to worship them.'"

Could God tell a man or woman to not get divorced after their spouse has cheated on them and liked doing it? Don't ask me. Ask Hosea. He will be the first to tell you that he loved the Lord, and his spouse. As a matter of fact, he was very clear that God told him to marry this person. God told him up front in Chapter 1 that his wife had some issues before they were married, and that those issues would be a part of their marriage. So, the sex issue manifests itself in the marriage, the wife leaves to run the streets, and Hosea is left to take care of the kids! Now, after all of that trauma he went through, surely God would give him a free pass to move on and get a divorce right? Wrong! He tells him to take his own money, and buy back his wife! God really must be crazy, huh? Not so. He told Hosea that the marriage wasn't all about him. His marriage was an example to Israel of how He loved them through all of their issues and unfaithfulness. He had a covenant with Israel, not a contract. He really means for better or for worse. So are there relationships that can stand tests like this today? Only when God has given clarity that the two should be together and only when they both recognize they both have issues going in. Most importantly, the two must recognize that God doesn't deserve to be cheated on, hurt, neglected, not spoken to, go days without hearing we love Him, or to have over things chosen over Him. Yet, we have done and still do those things, and He works with us, forgives us, and doesn't divorce us. He challenges us, disciplines us, and His anointing may leave us, but we still belong to Him in relationship. Is God crazy? Nope. But humans can miss the meaning of what He is trying to do in us, and in our relationships, when we focus on ourselves as if we have never disappointed Him without any fault of His. Friend, are you willing to hear God as He relates to your relationship decisions, or will you make the decision you feel you deserve? Loving like God is no joke. Is it in you?

Prayer: Dear Jesus, help us hear clearly from You before we make any relationship decisions, especially about getting married or getting divorced. If You call two people to be together, then the relationship is not just about their happiness, but about a message You are trying to show Your people as it relates to Your love toward us. Help us to not move until we have heard clearly from You even when we have been hurt. In Jesus' name I pray, Amen.

Questions

1. Have you been in a relationship where the person told you upfront about his/her issues, and when they arose you could handle them? Why or why not?

2. Are there times when you look back over your relationships and think that you could have handled it differently and wish you had one more chance? When and why?

3. Are you willing to hear God as He relates to your relationship decisions, or will you make the decision you feel you deserve? Why?

4. Before you take another step in your relationships, what can you focus on so you may be a ministry to others and to your partner?

"Respect And Love, Love And Respect"

Ephesians 5:33 "So again I say, each man must love his wife as he loves himself, and the wife must respect her husband."

Relationships can be a challenge at every stage. They will never be perfect, but they can get better as each individual involved remembers to display two words to one another regardless of how they feel, but based on what is right and what they committed to. Many marriages suffer today because these two words never have time to develop strong enough in the dating relationship. We tend to make decisions about our relationships based more on what we feel we need and what a person can bring to us, rather than what we can offer them, even if they do something with which we disagree. What are these two words? Love and respect. Why date someone you don't respect? Why marry someone you really don't love? Why commit to someone you really don't love? Yet people do it every single day. God commands husbands to love their wives and women (wives) to respect their husbands. It wasn't a suggestion. Some keywords we must look at in this verse show why people can't perform this command. "Each man must love his wife." The keyword is man! Boys aren't mature enough to sacrifice, take the time to communicate their feelings, and ask for forgiveness even when a woman has hurt them with her words or actions. Only real men can do that. Not to say that they don't get frustrated, but they always work through it! "The wife must respect her husband." Keyword: wife! This requires her being a real woman and lady. A real woman and lady knows that one of the greatest needs of a man is respect. She also knows that even if she can't respect her husband because of the love she doesn't feel by his actions, she respects his position as her husband even when he doesn't deserve it because it takes Jesus' kind of love. This is when you give something to a person even when they don't deserve it. That's what He does to us everyday. The sad fact is, people generally have a hard time showing respect or giving love to one another when we don't see what we are getting out of it.

Friend, if you don't want to grow then don't get into a relationship because they will challenge you everyday to grow up or not act like a child. You are getting out of it an opportunity to show Christ you want to really grow up to love like Him even when it hurts like He did on the cross. (We ain't ready for that. The pain we feel is that of a mere scratch compared to nails in the hand.) Relationships that last and are healthy are relationships that honor their commitment to show love and respect. By the time you finish dating with that mindset, you'll see if you can love and respect that person till death do you part. Are you single? How has your showing of love and respect in relationships been? Are you married? You made the choice, now God is holding you accountable to what you told Him you would do! He doesn't feel sorry for us, but is challenging us to think before we decide to marry or divorce. Think about it. Two words are the root to our problems. Just make sure you have done your part before you decide to depart.

Prayer: Dear Jesus, I pray that You give us wisdom and tougher skin so we can show love and respect the way You have shown it to us, though we never deserve it! In Jesus' name I pray, Amen.

Questions

1. Have you ever dated someone whom you did not respect or did not love, but liked? Why did you stay in the relationship? Be honest.

2. Can you really call yourself a "man" or a "wife" as described in this lesson? Why or why not?

3. While in your relationships, or if you want to be in one, are you willing to have an opportunity to show Christ you want to really grow up to love like Him even when it hurts like He did on the cross. Why or why not?

4. How can you focus on showing wisdom, love, and respect to others before you decide to marry or divorce someone?

"Don't Make Time For Haters"

Nehemiah 6:3 "...so I replied by sending this message to them: 'I am engaged in a great work, so I can't come. Why should I stop working to come to meet with you?'"

In life, there will be times when you are called to do something either no one else can do, is willing to do, or wants to see done for whatever reason. Once you begin to make progress, all of a sudden you will attract all types of individuals to the very thing you were trying to build. That thing you were trying to build could be your self esteem, business, or just your life in general.

Such is the situation with Nehemiah rebuilding the city wall of Jerusalem. No one thought it could be done; however, when it was being done- successfully at that - he attracted haters who were intimidated because they saw the walls almost complete and the gaps had been filled. As long as you are empty, people don't hate on you, but when God gives you the ability to fill in the gaps, well, that's just too much for some people to handle. They hate on you because they are empty and you are now full. Has God filled in any gaps for you lately? That means everyone isn't happy. Nehemiah teaches us how to respond to certain people who act like they want to meet you for the right reason, but really have no good intentions planned for you.

1. So I replied sending this message to them. Sometimes, you need to give a response, not out of anger, but out of confidence, that you know who you are, and you know who they are. Avoiding the situation sometimes will signal that you may be afraid.

2. I am engaged in a great work. Sometimes you need to state the obvious - first, before they try to minimize it - so they can see that you are aware of the importance of what you are doing. Nehemiah let them know he knew his work was a great responsibility and had great potential. In other words, what he was doing was important and they knew it, but he had to let them know again before they opened their mouths.

3. So I can't come. At times, you have to decline invitations, no matter who invites you, when you know they mean you no good and don't like what you stand for.

4. Why should I stop working to come to meet with you? Be aware of distractions. Sometimes Satan will invite you to a meeting or an event that may be grand. People would love to go to the places you have just been invited to, but you have to ask yourself the same question Nehemiah asked himself and of those who were hating on him: "Why should I stop working to come to meet with you?" Sometimes, the invitation is an invitation to stop you from working so the enemy can start destroying your confidence and stall the progress of what you were trying to build. Be careful of taking breaks when a task is almost complete. Sometimes it isn't necessary.

Friend, keep on building. Sometimes you don't need to waste

time explaining to people what you are trying to build. If they don't have a hammer and nails in their hand then they don't plan on helping you build anything anyway. Keep it moving! **If people's conversation can't sustain your vision, they may be there to drain your vision!** Beware of vision drainers. They are haters who don't want to see you succeed. Listen to Nehemiah and your walls will be complete sooner than you think. Keep on building! Make today a hater free day. Let them know you don't have room on your calendar for hateration. They need to reschedule their appointment! Then, enjoy your new progress.

Prayer: Dear Jesus, teach us to build in the midst of those who only want to tear down. In Jesus' name I pray, Amen.

Questions

1. Have there been times during a project when your focus was broken and you had difficulty finishing what you had worked so hard to complete? Have you finished that project? Why not?

2. Do you find it hard to decline invitations no matter who invites you? Why?

3. When you are building things in your life, do you find that the same people are doubting your ability, or what the Lord told you? Identify them and ask yourself why they resist your growth.

4. If the causes of you losing your focus on the project are still in your life, what do you need to do to get back on course?

"Living A Lover's Life"

Philippians 1:9-10 "So this is my prayer: that your love will flourish and that you will not only love much but well. Learn to love appropriately. You need to use your head and test your feelings so that your love is sincere and intelligent, not sentimental gush. Live a lover's life, circumspect and exemplary, a life Jesus will be proud of..." (The Message Translation)

Loving people can be a challenging and tiresome task. When you don't really know how to love, it can be even more frustrating and fearful. Whatever side of the fence you find yourself on as it pertains to loving others, make sure you do love. Paul prays for the Philippians and their love for one another. I extend this prayer and its principles to you today.

1. That your love will flourish and that you will not only love much, but well. Our love is supposed to grow, bloom, and blossom. Make sure you don't put limits on how much you love. Someone needs your love. Love much! Don't just love much, love WELL! Love until people can't take it anymore! Love until tears come from their eyes and yours. Love WELL!

2. Learn to love appropriately. We must learn to love. Everyone must LEARN to love. Some are quick studies. Others have to learn how to set boundaries, how to open up, how to be more giving, how to communicate, and how to be less selfish. That is the beauty of relationships; they challenge you to grow. The sad thing is, if you don't grow you will be soon ready to go! Maybe relationships get more challenging because our growth in an area is about to blossom. Before you go, think. Why? It may just be time to grow! I know you think you know all about love, but you don't. EVERYONE still has so much to learn. Maybe we need to GROW UP in order to really love properly.

3. You need to use your head and test your feelings so that love is sincere, intelligent, and not sentimental gush. God doesn't want us in dumb love! You have to use your heart AND mind when you love people. Thinking is a part of loving. If you don't think, how do you really know something? In order to get saved, you had to "believe in your heart and confess with your mouth." In order to believe, you had to think. God wants us to think and feel so we can love with intelligence. You can love someone who doesn't love you at all. If you just are going by feelings, that's not smart love. You may need to love them from a distance! **Think! Is this really love?**

4. Live a lover's life, circumspect and exemplary, a life of which Jesus will be proud. Loving people should be a lifestyle. How's your love life? Can Jesus be proud of how you are loving others? If you are not loving yourself and Jesus properly, how can He be proud of that? If you are loving Jesus and yourself properly, it usually shows up in the health of your love relationships. Make Jesus proud by showing some love!

How's your love life?

Prayer: Dear Jesus, teach me how to love with my mind, body, and soul in a way that makes You proud. In Jesus' name I pray, Amen.

Questions

1. Do you find loving others to be a tiresome and frustrating task, or do you find the challenge helping you to grow? Why?

2. Do you find that you give or show love to others because you want to or because you feel you have to? Are you cheerful when you love?

3. Is Jesus proud of how you are loving others? Why or why not?

4. How can you focus on learning to love others so that they not only receive the love, but that the Lord is proud of you?

"A Challenge And Warning For Men To Remain Faithful"

Proverbs 5:15 "Drink water from your own well - share your love only with your wife." (New Living Translation)

King Solomon had 700 wives and 300 girlfriends (concubines). He pauses to give counsel to a young man in Proverbs about being a man and dealing with women. He should know! Being a godly man is not an easy task, but is one that is full of challenges.

Knowing this, Solomon thought it necessary to encourage as well as challenge this man in Proverbs Chapter 5 to do his best to remain faithful to his wife because God was watching and wanted the best for him. There are consequences to being unfaithful. This was written centuries ago, yet Solomon seemingly knew there were some things that would always be a challenge to a godly man: being faithful to God, and to his wife. Let's read Proverbs 5:15-23 and see if this remains true today. Be encouraged, my brother. Let's strengthen one another while the sisters pray our strength to be what God called us to be. This is for husbands, and husbands in training.

1. If God has given/blessed you with a queen, only be her king. Drink water from your own well. Share your love only with your spouse. Why spill the water of your springs in the streets, having sex with just anyone?

2. If you are a wife, be a fountain of blessings to your man. Make sure you're not empty when he needs to be refreshed because you will leave him thirsty. That thirst still needs to be quenched. You should reserve it for yourselves never to share it with strangers. Let your wife be a fountain of blessings for you.

3. Enjoy the wife God gives you. If you give her attention you may see she is more loving and beautiful than you thought. Rejoice in the wife of your youth. She is a loving deer, a graceful doe.

4. Self Explanatory! Let her breasts satisfy you always. May you always be captivated by her love.

5. Although you could think of some reasons why you should cheat, what type of woman would cheat with you as opposed to the character of your wife? Obviously not one you would marry 9 times out of 10! Why be captivated, my son, by an immoral woman, or fondle the breasts of a promiscuous woman?

6. Your wife doesn't know, the neighbors don't know, the kids don't know, but God does. For the Lord sees clearly what a man does, examining every path he takes. An evil man is held captive by his own sins; they are ropes that catch and hold him.

7. You may get by, but you won't get away in the end. He will die for lack of self control; he will be lost because of his great foolishness.

If Solomon is wrong, cheating is right and there are no consequences. If Solomon is right, we have to battle our flesh, fend off loose women, and do our best to be better men in the area of faithfulness.

Don't you want to be a better man? I do. Ladies, don't you want better men to choose from? Issue the challenge in love. Men, let's fight to rise to the challenge for the love of God, family, children, and ourselves. Otherwise, are we really real men or boys with manly responsibilities? Be encouraged, my brother.

Prayer: Dear Jesus, help us to be the godly men you desire us to be. Help us be better for our families, communities, churches, and ourselves. When we are weak and tempted, give us the strength to remember the consequences. In Jesus' name I pray, Amen.

Questions

1. Being a godly man, what are some of the challenges you have being faithful?

2. Wife: Are You a blessing to your husband? Single Lady: How can you grow to become a blessing to the man the Lord will send to you? Husband: Are you allowing your wife to be a blessing to you?

3. Men: Do you have a lack of self-control? Women: Do you allow your men to be out of control? Why?

4. How can you focus being the person that the Lord and you desire you to be? What distractions do you need to remove or actions you need to add to your life?

"Single Or Married?" (Part 1)

1 Corinthians 7:32-34 "I want to free you from the concerns of this life. An unmarried man can spend his time doing the Lord's work and thinking how to please Him. But a married man has to think about earthly responsibilities and how to please his wife. His interests are divided."

There was a time not long ago when you were given an option of how you wanted to leave the grocery store on your way home that evening. They would ring you up and simply ask, "Paper or Plastic?" The decision you made was mostly based on how much usage you could get out of the bag, long or short term. Both served their initial purpose of simply getting your goods safely together to your vehicle and into your home. You would not be concerned about your goods that were valuable to you falling on the ground and becoming ruined right before your eyes because you felt what you chose would protect them and keep them together. You thought they would be stable enough.

Remaining single or getting married are options God allows us to choose between in life. There are consequences for either choice, but we must make the decision we believe God wants us to choose. There are goods inside of us, and if we choose to let the wrong person handle them they could utterly end up on the ground right before our eyes broken and fragmented needing restoration and healing. That's why it is very important for us to understand what God says through the Apostle Paul about singleness and marriage.

1. "I want to free you from the concerns of this life." Paul let us know that both marriage and singleness are "gifts" not "curses" from God. (I Corinthians 7:7) Maybe you haven't enjoyed your gift because you haven't opened the box yet! However, many individuals are all tied up and worried about trying to get married or get divorced. Marriage is only for the earth. There is no marriage in Heaven. That is only a concern for this life. God wants us not to worry over things in this life. If it happens, it happens. Free yourself. Don't make it happen if God didn't approve it for you. Worry doesn't make time, it wastes time. It's a battle in your mind, but do battle.

2. "An unmarried man can spend his time doing the Lord's work and thinking how to please Him." A single man has time to focus on growing in the Lord, utilizing his gifts, talents, and abilities to bring more souls to the kingdom. He is free to move, and go about as he pleases. However, if he is spending all of his time focusing on pleasing himself, he is wasting his single life, and will be hell to deal with when or if he gets married. If he doesn't use single moments for growth, giving, developing and reaching goals, and God, he will be more of a selfish, unfocused, stagnant, and immature person spiritually. "DOING THE LORD'S WORK" must be included while you are making money as a single. Enjoy your freedom, but make sure you aren't single in status, but bound in spirit to the wrong things. That can be dangerous.

3. "But a married man has to think about his earthly responsibilities and how to please his wife." If a single man gets married, he now must realize he is not just focused on himself. He no longer is responsible just for himself. He now has **"earthly responsibilities."** Part of the responsibility, a major part, is **"how to please his wife."** If he spent no preparation time before marriage understanding what a husband is, what a wife is, how to please her while he was dating her before marriage, he will struggle greatly in this area. If he marries a woman who does not really know what it means to be a wife, his job is intensified! If his wife is not spiritual, and doesn't like church or growing in Christ, it just became ten times harder. However, that is part of his responsibility now. No need in belly aching. Get on your job! It's too late now to want someone in Christ now that you recognize cute wears off!

4. "His interests are divided." The focus, attention, freedom you had in Christ to give Him everything, is tempered when you are not married to someone who has your same desire for Him. You have to please her and please Christ. That means you can't please Christ without pleasing her because you are to love her like Christ loved the church. That also means, your first ministry now is at home. If she is more focused on houses, cars, clothes, and trips than serving, growing, tithing, sacrificing and the like, she's still yours. And yes, the rule still applies for loving her like Christ loves the church. Your interests are "divided." If she is growing with you, life can be great. If she is not, it can be gruesome.

So, stay single or get married? Either way, make sure you read the fine print and take responsibility for whom you choose. Choose responsibly.

Prayer: Dear Jesus, help us to appreciate the state You have allowed us to be in. If married, thank You. If single, thank You. Help us see the gift in either situation so we can celebrate the gift. In Jesus' name I pray, Amen.

Questions

1. Single: are you a selfish, unfocused, stagnant, immature person spiritually? What can you do to grow? Engaged or Married Person: Have you grown out of these ways? If not, why and how can you become mature in these areas?

2. When you chose or are choosing a spouse, what are the things you want them to focus on in the relationship? If you have someone in your life, have you expressed this to them?

3. Single: Are you preparing to be able to please your wife? Married: Are you taking responsibility in your role as a husband and nurturing your marriage? How?

4. Being single or married, how can focus on growing in the Lord, utilizing your gifts, talents and abilities to bring more souls to the kingdom, and establishing and improving your relationship (ministry) as a reflection of how the Lord loved the church?

"Single Or Married?"
(Part 2)

1 Corinthians 7:34-35 "In the same way, a woman who is no longer married or has never been married can be devoted to the Lord and holy in body and spirit. But a married woman has to think about her earthly responsibilities and how to please her husband. I am saying this for your benefit, not to place restrictions on you. I want you to do whatever will help you serve the Lord best, with as few distractions as possible."

Let's start Part 2 from a woman's perspective as we did in Part 1 for the men and look at the scriptures.

1. "A woman who is no longer married or has never been married can be devoted to the Lord" Unless she has been bruised or had some very poor role models, the average woman is very devoted once she makes a commitment to a man. That faithfulness will carry her through good times, and bad times with an individual. You can see this with a mother loving her children. No matter how awful everyone else thinks they are, she remains devoted. While single or no longer married, she has time to give that same devotion to the things of God. God expects her to be devoted to Him even more than she would be devoted to any man that came into her life. God is good, faithful, consistent, honest, and a great communicator. To not be faithful to Him, and not do what He says is a slap in His face when you show more devotion to a man who makes mistakes and fails you.

2. "In body and spirit" A single woman can be devoted with her body fully to God, and that is what He desires. Sex before marriage is so powerful in this sense. A woman cannot give up her body without opening up her spirit. The person who has her body is the same person who has her spirit. That is why it is **easier** to walk away from a relationship when there has been no sex involved for the woman. When her body gets involved, her emotions and devotion get involved as well. That's why God wants to reserve that for Himself until He gives her away in marriage.

3. "But a married woman has to think about her earthly responsibilities and how to please her husband." If a single woman gets married, she now must realize she is not just focused on herself. She no longer is responsible just for herself; she now has "**earthly responsibilities.**" Part of the responsibility, a major part, is "**how to please her husband.**" If she spent no preparation time before marriage understanding what a husband is, what a wife is, how to please him while she was dating him before marriage, she will struggle greatly in this area. If she marries a man who does not really know what it means to be a husband, her job is intensified! If her husband is not spiritual, and doesn't like church or growing in Christ, it just became ten times harder. However, that is part of her responsibility now. No need in belly aching. Get on your job! It's too late now to want someone in Christ now that you recognize cute wears off!

Being in church alone gets old. Not wanting to have sex because he's not spiritual enough is not okay with God. It is your "**earthly responsibility**" regardless!

4. "I want you to do whatever will help you serve the Lord best, with as few distractions as possible." God desires you to serve Him whether single or married. It is evident that when you are married there are distractions. However, if you marry a man who is immature, self centered, lazy, won't lead like he is supposed to, won't take you to church or lead prayer at home, will live with you, but will not lead you the right way and marry you which is what a real godly man will do, you will be distracted. You can't really give to God when you're always complaining when you want to do spiritual things. You will be distracted when you are worshiping in church with part of your brain, and the other part is heartbroken because you want to share that experience with him now that you are growing. Part of your heart is with God, the other with your man because they are in two different places.

So my friend, are you going to stay single, get married or rekindle the love you once had in your marriage? Either way, make sure you read the fine print and take responsibility for whom you choose. Choose responsibly.

Prayer: Dear Jesus, help us to appreciate the state in which You have allowed us to be. If married, thank You. If single, thank You. Help us see the gift in either situation so we can celebrate the gift. In Jesus' name I pray, Amen.

Questions

1. Are you totally committed to the Lord? How do you know and what is your gauge to let you know you are?

2. Single Lady: Do you find it hard to walk away from a relationship once it ends? Do you understand why after reading Section 2? What can you do to give your whole body back to Christ? Married Lady: Do you still find it hard to fully commit your body to your husband due to a break up? What can you do to heal?

3. Single: Are you preparing to be able to please your husband? Married: Are you taking responsibility in your role as a wife by nurturing your marriage and not being a distraction? How?

4. Whether single or married, how can you focus on growing in the Lord, utilizing your gifts, talents and abilities to bring more souls to the kingdom, and establishing and improving your relationship (ministry) as a reflection of how the Lord loved the church?

"How To Survive A Breakup"

Acts 27:44 "The others held onto planks or debris from the broken ship. So everyone escaped safely to shore."

Headlines read: **Air France jet debris recovered.**

The control tower watched as over two hundred passengers and crew boarded Air France. None of them expected what happened in the midst of their flight. They were soaring at great altitudes and having normal conversation when, all of a sudden, all communication ceased. The only thing the control tower knows is that the plane disappeared from the grid, began losing altitude, and began to break up in mid flight. All that was left was debris scattered over a 3 mile area. The black boxes that stored the information and held the truth about what really took place may be over 22,000 feet deep in the watery area the plane is projected to have crashed. No one may ever know what really caused the breakup to occur, but they have enough evidence to speculate. There were no survivors.

Many times, like Air France, relationships take drastic turns. You can be excited about your wonderful trip together, communication seems to be flowing well, and you trust the other person with your life. Then, out of nowhere, your relationship begins to lose altitude, go to a place that you can't understand, the communication fails, and all you have left are pieces to pick up with no information as to what really took place. Your relationship black box seems to be buried so far in someone's heart or mind that you may never really understand what took place.

Some relationships end that way. The reality is, you may never truly understand what happened. You have to pick up the pieces and adjust your life little by little and decide to continue to live and love again. It's a difficult process, but it is a necessary one if you are going to make the best of your life.

The Apostle Paul was on a ship that had broken up as well. There were two ways that individuals were able to survive this broken situation:

1. **"Then he ordered all who could swim to jump overboard first, and make for land."** (vs. 43) Sometimes you have to jump out of some things while you see them falling apart before they take you down. You may have to leave some things in your boat, but your life is more important. God taught you how to swim. Swim to another place and start over. If it is a marriage, think twice before jumping. You need clearance from God for sure because marriage is not like dating. Marriage is biblical and held to a higher standard by God.

2. **"The others held onto planks or debris from the broken ship. So everyone escaped safely to shore."** (vs. 44) You may be the one not strong enough to swim because you are so hurt and broken. Just hold on to something. Use the broken pieces as a vehicle to get you to where you need to be. Don't drown! Hold on to God like

never before while you are seemingly in dangerous waters, not knowing where you are or what to do now.

Yes, sometimes breakups come seemingly out of nowhere. Other times you can see them coming. Sadly, some have broken up and did not survive. If you are still alive, monitor your flight, and analyze your ship. If you have time to make a decision, make one. If you didn't have time and it was made for you, make a decision to live! The people on that flight didn't have a chance. God allowed it to take place for some reason we may never know. Sometimes that's what happens with our relationships. If they left you alive, thank God for the positive memories, but now it is time to build some new ones.

Prayer: Dear Jesus, I pray for those who have had relationships break up and they don't know what to do, whether it was recent or a few years ago. I pray that You give them new perspectives on life, heal their hearts and minds, then help them not to spend so much time on why, but turn to the ONE WHO can make their next trip in life ten times better than the last. In Jesus' name I pray, Amen.

Questions

1. Do you have an understanding of why there were breakups in your past? What was the cause of the break up?

2. Were you able to and did you grow and learn from those experiences? Why or why not? Are you still healing?

3. Have you healed so that you can fully love the next person the Lord places into your life? Do you still have debris from a past relationship that need to be collected, surveyed, and destroyed?

4. How can you focus on creating a new perspective on your life, allow time to heal your heart and mind, and not spend so much time wondering why it happened, but accepting that the Lord allowed it to happen?

"Why Are You So Attractive?"

Matthew 4:19 "Come follow me, and I will show you how to fish for people."

What attracts you? Better yet, who seems to be attracted to you? Did you know there is a reason why certain people like your style, and others don't? I know there are some people you wish had never even noticed you. You are trying to get rid of some even as you read this, right?

Jesus, in our text, challenges the disciples to follow Him. Then, He lets them know that He will teach them how to attract people for the right reasons. It seems that because they were fishermen, they knew something about putting the right bait on a hook in order to draw the attention of a fish. Jesus flips the script on the ones He had chosen, and not only made them the fishermen, but indirectly lets them know they were the bait, too!

The reason certain people are attracted to you and want to get to know you, even sometimes when you haven't the slightest interest in them, is because you're bait! God has put something ON YOU, but it is your responsibility to have something that is godly IN YOU to say to them when you speak with them. The word of encouragement, the Gospel Message, or positive information from the Bible.

What would happen if all the people who tried to get your

phone number or tried to ask you on a date got saved? What if God allowed them to come to you so you could give them a message from Him? What would happen if we talked as much about having a healthy growing relationship with Christ as much as we talk to others about a business deal we are trying to close? What would happen if we had more phone numbers in our pocket from the club that we went to in order to follow up on those who we had just witnessed to rather than ask on a date? What would happen if we started looking at our pests as potential Christians? What would happen if you turned someone down for a deal or a date, but then said, "But there is something I do want to talk with you about?" And then you give them a word of encouragement rather than look at them crazy? Please don't beat them over the head and drown them in scripture. Just encourage them.

The truth is, we are only attractive physically, financially, socially, or spiritually because God allows us to be. Some of it is to get you a date, but most of it is to attract others to set them up on a date with destiny!

Here's my challenge to you today, friend: when someone comes to you wanting to hold a conversation and get to know you, ask that person a few simple questions:

> **"I'm just curious to know, friend…**

1. **Are you in love with Jesus like I am?"** Then if he/she asks what you mean ask…

2. **Do you have about a minute for me to tell you why I am in love with Him?"** If he/she says yes, then say, "I deserved to go to hell, but He told

me I didn't have to if I accepted His offer of a relationship that would last forever. I did, and I have been loving Him ever since and desire for others to feel love like this, too. I have security, peace, and I trust Him. There isn't a better relationship than this! If you don't have this love you can get it by doing what I did!" Then, if that person asks "How?" reel 'em in! Read, study, and meditate on your scriptures, and you will be ready to lead others to Christ.

Remember: We are bait and fishermen. Once they come to you, reel 'em in! You can't force it on them. Just share and let God do the rest. Use whatever catches people's attention to God's advantage and God will make sure it works for your advantage! You thought you were just gifted and cute for you, huh? Sorry friend...Wrong Answer! It's all for His glory. Let Him use you.

Prayer: Dear Jesus, help us see people as You do. You see them as Your creation which needs Your love regardless of what they have done and where they have been. Teach us how to fish and be bait that not only is attractive to others, but attractive to You first. In Jesus' name I pray, Amen.

Questions

1. How often do you speak of the Lord or witness to someone?

2. As asked in your devotion, what would happen if you turned someone down for a deal or a date, but then said, "But there is something I do want to talk with you about"?

3. Are there any factors that prohibit you from witnessing? (It's not allowed at work, you're not secure enough to answer questions when witnessing, you do not feel you are called, etc.)

4. What do you need to focus on to become better bait and a better fisherman?

"We Need To Talk"

1 Peter 3:1-2 "In the same way, you wives must accept the authority of your husbands. Then, even if some refuse to obey the Good News, your godly lives will speak to them without any words. They will be won over by observing your pure and reverent lives."

The headlines read: **Woman Tries to Keep Husband...With Handcuffs!**

A woman handcuffed herself to her husband while he was asleep. She also had changed the locks on the doors. When the police arrived after he called 911, they heard screams coming from their bedroom; she was biting him on his arms and torso. When asked why she did all of this, she replied, "I wanted to have a conversation without him leaving." She was trying to reconcile with him.

Communication is important in relationships, but we need to make sure we take sane measures in order to accomplish our goals! I admire this lady for her desire to communicate and work on her marriage. Although it was too extreme, it does drive the point home that if you are in a relationship, you should make it a point to not go anywhere at times until you have an understanding and have clearly communicated.

Ladies, I know you get frustrated when men don't want to talk; however, Peter gives us a less severe way to win him over in order to accomplish effective communication wherein you do not have to manipulate or force him to do so. "Your godly lives will speak to them without any words. They will be won over by observing your pure and reverent lives." This lady's actions were not pure and certainly were not reverent. She wanted control and would go to dramatic lengths in order to try to achieve her goal, and the only thing it got her were the following charges: third degree assault, disorderly conduct, reckless endangerment, and unlawful restraint! Needless to say, she still didn't get what she needed and made matters even worse. She made herself look like a fool while bringing her neighbors and the police into a private matter.

Gentleness goes a long way. Peter says her "life will speak without words." Sometimes, actions do speak louder than words. The next time you want your man to speak and he doesn't, maybe you need to let your actions speak louder than your words in a godly, reverent way. Learn to speak another language. This goes not only for women, but for men as well. Forcing people to talk is what terror experts are trained to do with prisoners. Giving people the time and opportunity to talk is what respectful, patient, loving people in relationship do. Yes, it's frustrating to wait at times, but how long did God have to wait for you before you started talking to Him like He wants you to? Think about it, friend.

Meditation Scriptures: Ephesians 4:17-31

Prayer: Dear Jesus, help our actions speak louder than our words, and when they speak, help them speak in a reverent, godly manner that will encourage others to want to open up and dialogue with us. In Jesus' name I pray, Amen.

Questions

1. Think about how you communicate with others. Do you do so with action or with words? Why?

2. Rank your ways of communicating: cell phone (voice or text), your computer (email or Skype), face-to-face, or by office and home phone? Why do you use more of the top ranked than the lesser?

3. Due to technology, have you found that your personal (face-to-face) communication skills and showing/giving time, love, and affection have diminished?

4. What can you do to show you cherish and welcome the time to communicate effectively so you can focus on enhancing your relationships?

"Miracle Mama"

John 2:3&5 "The wine supply ran out during the festivities, so Jesus' mother spoke to Him about the problem. 'They have no more wine,' she told Him. But His mother told the servants, 'Do whatever He tells you.'

We often remember that Jesus' first miracle was turning water into wine, but sometimes we miss the fact that His mama believed that her Child had miracle-working power in Him before He ever performed one miracle, and she challenged Him to let it out. That's why I call Mary a "Miracle Mama". When you think about it, mamas do work miracles.

My mom used to take two salmon croquettes and some Wonder Bread and feed five family members. Mama used spit on her finger, and clean the corner of my eyes so I could see. My mama used to lay hands on the sick kids in the house and we would recover after falling down outside or bruising our knees. My mama could take a chicken when we had little money and make it last a whole week by frying it, baking it, putting it in sandwiches, and much more. Mama could send me to college and make sure my financial needs were taken care of (before I could help out by helping my siblings and her and my dad's current responsibilities), work the midnight shift on her job, come home and cook breakfast, get us dressed for church, teach Sunday School, sing in the choir, cook dinner, spend time with us, and go back to work that night. My mama could look at us in the middle of a church service and we'd miraculously understand expressions that meant, "I'm gonna get you when we get home if you don't stop talking in church!"

Like Mary, my mama could, and still can tell me things that I need to do or things that are about to change in my life, while I haven't talked with her about any of them. My mama can calm storms in my life by saying and praying, "Peace Be Still!" She may have been broke, in pain, or afraid, but the miracle was you may have never known how deep it was then because things still got done. Mamas do work miracles! You may have performed some great feats in life, and turned water into wine, but there isn't a finer wine than a mother who has been there for you when you didn't even know you needed her. Even if your mother has passed away, your life is the miracle that she left behind. Thank your mother for pushing you, encouraging you, challenging you, and loving you. The next time you think about her, remember she is a MIRACLE MAMA!

Prayer: Dear Lord, thank You for real mamas or the women who were in our lives as representations of mothers. The fact that we have mothers, and we're able to be born from their womb, in the flesh or in the spirit, is a miracle in itself. Help me recognize that I do what I do and I am who I am because I am a miracle that came through her because of You. In Jesus' name, Amen.

Questions

1. What is some of the best advice you have received from your mother or someone that was like a mother to you?

2. What lesson can you pass on to those who do not have mothers?

3. Besides celebrating your mothers on Mother's Day, how do you appreciate the mothers in your life?

4. How can the Lord guide you to be an influence to others who need motherly advice and guidance? (Even if you have not had children of your own or if you are a male, you can do this.)

Made in the USA
Monee, IL
07 July 2026

56552292R00095